D0058189

# IT'S TIME TO FIGHT DIRTY

★ ★ ★ ★

★ ★ ★ DAVID FARIS ★ ★ ★

# IT'S TIME TO FIGHT DIRTY

★ ★ ★ ★

## HOW DEMOCRATS CAN BUILD A LASTING MAJORITY IN AMERICAN POLITICS

IT'S TIME TO FIGHT DIRTY



First Melville House printing: April 2018

Melville House Publishing
46 John Street
Brooklyn, NY 11201
and
8 Blackstock Mews
Islington
London N4 2BT

mhpbooks.com
facebook.com/mhpbooks
@melvillehouse

ISBN: 978-1-61219-695-4
ISBN: 978-1-61219-696-1 (eBook)

Sample ballot from Center for Civic Design and Oxide Design, based on the Election Assistance Commission (EAC) ballot layout guidelines. Map of California courtesy of the author.

Design by Betty Lew

Printed in the United States of America

10 9 8 7 6 5 4 3 2 1

A catalog record for this book is available from the Library of Congress

For Sheerine, always

# Contents

## CONCLUSION:

# Introduction

Since the shocking election of Donald Trump as the forty-fifth president of the United States, a lively and at times acrimonious debate has raged in the big tent of the American left. On one side are those who believe the Democratic Party should make a play for Trump voters by emphasizing progressive policy issues that appeal to the white working class—trade agreements, job retraining programs, universal healthcare, a basic income, and more.[1] The idea that the Democrats must transform themselves into a continental European-style workers' party is particularly popular with members of the Democratic Socialists of America (DSA) and other supporters of Senator Bernie Sanders who believe, not without evidence, that he would have made a better general election candidate than Hillary Clinton.[2] Another faction, still clearly influential in the Democratic Party, believes that the path to a new majority runs through appealing to moderate, wealthy, suburban Republicans who are disgusted by Trump and abandoning "identity politics."[3] Still others believe that the party just needs to stay the course—to get its base of women, minorities, and young people to the polls in numbers similar to 2008 and 2012, and that pivoting to Trump voters will alienate their most reliable supporters.[4] At times these competing visions have erupted into open warfare, with left-on-left Twitter looking like Day 110 of the Battle of the Somme, and at others they have led to vicious post-hoc recriminations about strategy, as when the DSA and its allies scoffed at Democratic candidate Jon Ossof's cautious, noncombative strategy in the Georgia House special election that took place in June 2017.[5]

In *It's Time To Fight Dirty*, I argue that *all* of the participants in this intra-left kerfuffle are failing to take the structural barriers to progressive power in this country seriously enough. Democrats will not build lasting power by landing on the right health care policy, or concocting the zingiest slogan, or targeting their last few million dollars in GOTV to this or that county in North Carolina. In fact, focusing only on policy or messaging or outreach would be a catastrophic mistake that will eventually land the party right back in the same position it is in now. It makes the error of believing that American politics is all about, or even mostly about, policy differences between the contenders for public office. But you cannot win, in the long term, a policy or messaging fight on a playing field that is tilted hopelessly against you. You can sometimes come out on top in a football game in which you spot your opponents two touchdowns before the game begins, but, and this is critical, *you will lose more often than you win*. If Democrats and progressives decide to duel to the death, particularly while they are in the minority, over whether the federal minimum wage should be $13 or $15, they will do so from the political sidelines, as their adversaries in the GOP continued to use a rigged political system to exclude them from the conversation altogether.

The unfortunate truth is that voters are rarely able to make the link between the party in power and policies that benefit (or disadvantage) them. This means that even though millions of Americans may benefit from, for instance, the Affordable Care Act, they don't necessarily credit Democrats for their gains. As political scientists Daniel Galvin and Chloe Thurston argue, "It is difficult for constituencies to form, for example, when policies lack visibility or traceability to the government."[6] Suzanne Mettler has theorized contemporary policymaking as part of a "submerged state," where government's efforts are intertwined with market actors, tax incentives, and other complex mechanisms that have the result of confusing the public about which group of policymakers is responsible for delivering benefits to them. Such policies, as Mettler argues, "obscure government's role from the view of the general public, including those who number among their beneficiaries."[7] Voters are also unlikely to shift partisan preferences based on one party delivering some basket of policy goodies to them—far more likely is that their party loyalties will lead them to shift their policy preferences away from those being offered by the other side. This is how, for example, you get late night comedians corralling Trump voters who think Obamacare and the Affordable Care Act are different things.[8] Overall, fully 35 percent of the public doesn't know that these terms refer to the same law.[9] And indeed, this lack of sophistication about policy led to an astonishing result in the 2016 election: "the positive correlation between geographical areas with the highest increases in enrollment for Obamacare and electoral support for Donald Trump in the 2016 election."[10]

Democrats didn't lose a policy fight in 2016. What they did was finish losing a procedural war that has been going on since the early 1990s. Indeed, the election of Donald Trump as the forty-fifth president of the United States was such an incomprehensible development that it obscured a very simple underlying reality: that the pathological liar and delusional narcissist currently residing half-time at the White House actually lost the presidential election by several million votes and took office because of the nonsensical, undemocratic Electoral College; that Democrats scored *11 million more votes* for the U.S. Senate than Republicans only to wake up staring at a 52–48 deficit; that the national House vote was nearly even but delivered Republicans yet another overwhelming majority; that of the 230 million voting-eligible citizens of the United States, fewer than 139 million even bothered to turn out; that millions of Americans were shamefully deprived of their franchise by racist voter-ID laws and the cruel way that many states prevent current or former felons from voting; and that the United States is the only country in the entire world that holds its critical national elections on a regular working Tuesday as if we literally couldn't care less who is able take off work to cast a ballot.

The bizarre quirks and preindustrial design features of the American constitutional system are in fact a five-star Epicurious recipe for how a radical minority of voters can capture and hold power in a democracy. These oddities almost exclusively favor the current voting coalition of the Republican Party, and GOP elites have ingeniously rolled out a long series of laws and court decisions to press their advantage—from the Citizens United atrocity that declared money is speech, to depraved voter ID laws that obviously target people who are likely to vote Democratic—all dressed up in Orwellian pabulum about free speech and the need to prevent voting fraud. Since the end of the Cold War, the Gingrich radicals that took over the party in the early 1990s have been waging a relentless, brutal, and completely one-sided war against the Democrats, systematically using their lawmaking power to disadvantage their adversaries in elections and political mobilization. As E. J. Dionne argues, these aggressive, norm-violating procedural moves were the hallmark of a party "determined to use the power it had to lock in its advantages for the future."[11] One has to grudgingly respect the single-mindedness with which the GOP has pursued its advantage in the electoral arena, even as we condemn the morally bankrupt disenfranchisement of voters and the ugly circus they have brought to Congress. Democrats would be wise to learn from their adversaries, even as they cling to a set of minimal behavioral standards.

That one-sided warfare, and the preposterous handicaps Democrats are forced to compete with, led directly to the election of Donald Trump. And on January 20, 2017, we began dealing with the consequences: When President Trump was inaugurated, he launched a gratuitous, mean-spirited, and corrupt assault on the governing norms of Washington, D.C. and the patterns and expectations of the American political system. Toting with him into office an unstable entourage of D-list hacks, cartoonish weirdos, and dead-eyed ideologues, Donald Trump arrived in D.C. to deliver an apocalyptic, angry inaugural speech that sounded like Ernest Hemingway's suicide note as interpreted by 4chan. In short, repetitive, declarative sentences, Trump proclaimed the end of "this American carnage" and promised that "from now on it will be America first, only America first."[12]

After the speech, former President George W. Bush—no intellectual titan himself—reportedly remarked, "That was some weird shit."[13] But it quickly became clear that "America First" was more of a threat issued by gangsters about the order of execution than a promise to improve the material conditions of the country. Barely twenty-four hours into his presidency, Trump set the tone for the entire four years by marching his blithering press secretary Sean Spicer in front of the cameras with pictures of the inauguration that looked like they'd been blown up at the Target photo center to insist that Trump had "the largest audience to ever witness an inauguration—period—both in person and around the globe."[14] The claim was belied by the evidence sitting right next to him on the podium and by a million first-hand pictures and videos and reports floating around the Internet, all of which showed a relatively sparsely attended inaugural. Those members of the press corps observing the spectacle got that feeling of listening to a wedding speaker slowly melt down, the guests glancing furtively at each other, mouthing "Is this really happening?"

To make matters worse, the political organization that folded for Trump and followed him gleefully into total power had completed a decades-long journey to the extreme right of the American political spectrum. The marauding Republican Party that rolled victoriously into D.C. in January 2017 had lost all sense of public spirit and graciousness and lacked utterly any reason for existing other than the relentless pursuit and maintenance of political power for the express purpose of redistributing wealth from the poor and the middle classes to the wealthy. In the first year of Trump's misrule, the GOP abdicated critical oversight functions and made excuse after excuse for the barely literate reality TV star in the Oval Office because they realized that they had a once-in-a-lifetime opportunity to reshape American public policy and deliver on the lurid and generally unpopular promises they have been making their voters for years, not just to repeal Obamacare but to dramatically roll back the scope of the federal government, gut the progressive tax code by drastically lowering rates for corporations and top earners, crush the remaining and embattled pockets of organized labor, obliterate environmental regulations while reanimating the zombie coal industry, and appoint constitutional fanatics to the United States Supreme Court. Most of these positions are profoundly unpopular. GOP elites know that they have a president elected with 46 percent of the vote, that they lost seats in both the House and Senate in 2016, and that long-term demographic trends do not work in their favor unless they can continually increase their share of the white vote. Many saw in Donald Trump a vehicle for a last-ditch effort to dismantle what hard-core conservatives refer to derisively as "the administrative state"—the network of federal and state civilian agencies that manage the many complexities of modernity so that all citizens have the opportunity to live a decent life amid the ravages of capitalism. This is why one writer and former George W. Bush apparatchik (who would, of course, be appointed to a position in the Trump Administration) described 2016 as "the Flight 93 election: charge the cockpit or you die."[15]

Such histrionic, This-Is-the-End readings of American politics are rarely correct, but Republican elites clearly felt that the election of Hillary Clinton, a careful, cautious technocrat with left-of-center but hardly radical views on most issues, would somehow tip the country into progressive authoritarianism. While they may have been wrong that a Clinton presidency would have been some kind of world-historical fulcrum point (a view that was decidedly *not* shared by the American left), on a deeper level they are right that American public opinion is moving slowly away from the market fundamentalism that has been the philosophy if not always the governing practice of the Republican Party since the late 1970s. Public opinion surveys suggest younger Americans are, for perhaps the first time in a century, open to being persuaded that government should play an even larger part in preventing capitalism from running amok. Seventeen- to thirty-four-year-olds in particular express much greater support for a government role in securing health care for all citizens and guaranteeing full employment than their older counterparts.[16]

Most worryingly for the GOP, millennials seem to support things like single-payer health care and more aggressive wealth-redistribution policies. Derided by their selfish elders, particularly the Baby Boomers, as flighty snowflakes with the attention spans of hamsters, millennials actually see straight through the lies told to them by a society dominated by conservatives since their parents were teenagers. They see that they are paying more and getting less than their parents, whether for college education or housing or medical care, and they are increasingly drawn to a social-democratic model whereby risk is pooled and an interventionist state makes public goods available for everyone in exchange for higher taxes. They are uninterested in casino capitalism. They are present and future progressives. The question posed by this book is whether these young progressives will ever live in a world where they are competing in a fair political fight with their conservative counterparts, or whether they think that new slogans or new policies will suffice.

If the first year of our national experiment in rule by Breitbart bloggers is any indication, Republicans stand a very good chance of delivering, through ineptitude, malice, and arrogance, power back to the Democrats in 2018 and 2020. President Trump plunged below Barack Obama's single worst Gallup approval rating number in a matter of weeks.[17] He was not wearing a bungee cord, and he's not coming back up. If Democrats can recruit a halfway decent cast of House and Senate candidates and manage not to restage the shootout scene in the season 2 finale of *Fargo* like they did in the 2016 primaries, they should wake up in January 2021 back in control of Congress and the presidency. The Democrats' overwhelming victories in the off-year 2017 elections—with Ralph Northam blowing out Republican Ed Gillespie for control of the Virginia governorship, Doug Jones edging out Republican Roy Moore for a Senate seat in Alabama of all places, and Democrats overperforming and making gains everywhere from the Washington State to Oklahoma—were the birds flying inland ahead of the incoming tsunami. The surge in women (including trans women) running successfully for office was particularly encouraging. The party must spend the next four years continuing to do the difficult and unglamorous work of recruiting quality candidates in races at every level of government, and giving them the financial and messaging support that they need to win their races and take back power from the GOP. Victory is not assured, but because President Trump and the Republicans appear intent on pursuing policy after policy that is opposed by decisive majorities of the American people, they stand an excellent chance at recapturing power in many states as well as staging their own takeover of Congress and the presidency. Yet their stay is likely to be just as miserably short-lived as their last stint in charge of the entire federal government between 2009 and 2011 if they do not consider making serious changes to the U.S. political system.

None of this is to suggest that Democrats should not vigorously pursue progressive public policy that will meaningfully impact the lives of their voters (and those who don't vote for them). But expecting a handful of policy victories in, say, the spring of 2021 to deliver multiple electoral cycles of victories to the Democrats is just a fantasy, and one that election results during the Obama era conclusively discredited. The stakes could not be higher: prevailing in the ugly spectacle of American elections has become a matter of life and death for everyone on the planet. If Democrats keep alternating power every four or eight years with the gaggle of climate-deniers and dirty-energy shills currently in charge of the Republican Party, all of our children are going to spend their golden years spit-roasting to death in a blistering hellscape that will make the plot of *Waterworld* look like a naïve aspiration. If a more competent version of this white nationalist circus is brought to power over the next decade, we could see the American democratic experiment wiped from the face of Earth. So it is not enough for the Democrats to sweep to power in 2020 by sitting back and letting Donald Trump wreck the country. It is not enough to score one or two overwhelming victories handed to us by a man determined to destroy his presidency and his party by putting his half-wit children and their mediocre spouses in charge of important national processes.

Instead, once back in control of Washington D.C., Democrats must use the very clear powers granted to them by the Constitution to pass laws addressing the shortcomings of the U.S. electoral system. Only by changing the rules that are currently rigged against them will Democrats ever hold power long enough to truly transform American politics in a lasting progressive direction. Doing so will require party leaders to pursue policy changes that will be ridiculed by their opponents as outrageous affronts to democratic decency and received by their own voters with puzzlement or even shock. They need to do it anyway. The shock will wear off. Luckily, many of these maneuvers don't need to be invented out of whole cloth—other democratic societies have devised workable solutions to the problems of getting people to vote and obliterating the obstacles that reactionaries cynically place between human beings and their ballot access. In other cases, such as the Democrats' structural disadvantage in the U.S. Senate, there are uniquely American remedies for our political problems. The thing that unites all of these potential procedural maneuvers is that few of them are much more complicated than passing laws in Congress and having them signed by the president.

While many people assume that critical features of our electoral politics are enshrined in the Constitution, few of them actually are. The Constitution is an extremely brief document that lays out some basic rules of the political order. It does not, however, have much to say on many features of our democracy that we take for granted. The size of the Supreme Court, the procedures we use to elect the House and how many people are elected, the number of states in the Union as well as the laws that govern who can vote and when are all issues about which the U.S. Constitution is mute. They developed instead over time, often accidentally or with little foresight about their long-term consequences. The beneficiaries of our democratic deficits developed ornate rationales for why, for instance, Washington, D.C. can't be a state or why we can never enlarge the House of Representatives ever again, as we did routinely during the nineteenth century. While such arguments are not completely meritless in every single case, for the most part they would not hold up in the face of a sustained Democratic political plan to change them, and importantly, most voters are indifferent at best to the whole field of electoral systems and political rules. If Democrats can draft these plans, have them vetted by the kind of competent, trained constitutional lawyers that the Trump administration can't seem to get its hands on, and have them ready to roll early in the next Democratic administration, they could functionally be implemented simultaneously, a kind of good-governance, electoral-systems blitzkrieg from which the Republican Party as currently constituted may never recover.

However, if this were just about improving the short-term fortunes of the Democratic Party, I would not be able to justify these recommendations to my own students. The reforms recommended in this book are, instead, designed to improve the long-term quality and performance of American representative democracy, and to bring our practices into line with innovations discovered elsewhere, or in some cases, recommended by the Framers themselves. If instituted as a bloc, they will improve access to the ballot, increase participation in our elections, decrease destructive tensions over the Supreme Court, mitigate the fundamental flaws of the Senate, bring members of the House closer to their constituents, and open the world of national politics to many more citizens. At the end of this process, Americans will despise their own politics a bit less, and feel more connected to the system. The point, of course, is not to institute single-party rule for the Democrats in perpetuity. It is to control the levers of power long enough to permanently alter the political trajectory of the country, to smash the current Republican coalition of misfit Nazi toys, misogynist creeps, and rich nihilists and replace it with a sensible, center-right opposition capable of telling the difference between fake news produced by Macedonian troll farmers and actual facts about the world that we inhabit together.

Some of the recommendations in this book will strike readers as so radical that they might precipitate a rupture of normal politics, or even a major constitutional crisis. Worrying about the damage these proposals might do is a genuinely adorable way to think about our politics, but it's kind of like fretting about whether you should shoot the terrorist sitting next to you on your flight after he's already blown a hole in the hull. We've been living through a major political crisis since the day that Barack Obama took office as the forty-fourth president of the United States, when the opposition party made a calculation that it would rather pursue and hold onto power than respect the vulnerable norms and procedures that make it possible for our government to function under divided government. More than anything, the Republican Party circa 2017 is an authoritarian minority party, clinging to power by abusing the clear spirit of the Constitution and benefitting from 200-year-old institutional design mistakes. The procedures that once guided bipartisan comity in the Senate—like the filibuster—are either on their way out or are already quite dead. Nor should they be mourned. The representative democracy that might emerge from this dispiriting period of total partisan war could actually be a significant improvement over what we have now. The difference between Republican and Democratic hardball is that for Republicans, the intent is to dismantle as much of the progress of the twentieth century as possible, to benefit rich people at the expense of literally everyone else in society. While the party was once clever enough to cloak this project in discredited economic theory and appeals to personal responsibility, the post-Trump iteration of America's robber baron political organization has seemingly misplaced its ability to even put clothes and makeup on its rotting corpse of an ideology.

For too long, Democrats have watched meekly while their opponents pass laws deliberately designed to smash their coalition (like the attempt to prevent unions from automatically collecting dues from all members), or whose obvious purpose is to make it harder for people who generally support Democrats to vote, or that deliberately use state policy to undermine sectors of society that fight on behalf of the people against powerful corporate interests. Republican leaders have consistently sought policy changes to deprive members of the Democratic coalition of their power in American society. What else could explain the Trump Administration's determination to gut a student loan repayment program that encourages, for instance, law school graduates to stay in the lower-paying public interest sector?[18] You know all those lawyers who rushed to the airports after Trump signed his idiotic Muslim ban in January 2017?[19] Many of them would not be able to continue the work they do if they had to repay their loans in full. There would be even fewer public defense attorneys, which we are already critically short on. Fewer people would choose to go into the public education sector.

All of these things would be just fine with the contemporary

GOP, which has fallen into the grasp of authoritarians who genuinely believe that there should be no check on the axis of corporate and carceral power possessed by the modern state. They understand that wielding power over your opponents like a cudgel is a much better bet than trying to win an argument with them. To see how and why this fight has been one-sided for a long time, imagine what it would look like if Democrats responded in kind in the realm of voting rights. If Democratic governors and legislatures wanted to drive down turnout in Republican areas, they might, for instance, close down voting stations in rural areas or pass laws forbidding gun licenses from being used as a valid form of identification at the polls. This would be horrible, right? Trying to prevent people from voting is a garbage tactic used by garbage human beings and Democrats should never do it, even if it gives them a momentary advantage. But this is what is being done to them. Over and over and over again. We've got all the Post-it notes and crime scene photos pinned to the wall like one of those tortured TV detectives, but we haven't connected the dots. The Right is out to destroy the Left as an organized force in American society. It really is that simple.

So what are my big ideas for how to fight back?

First, in chapter one, we'll take a little tour of America's expired milk carton of a founding document, the United States Constitution. Ingenious for its time, if deeply morally flawed, the Constitution saddles the country with a series of difficult political problems. Some are explicit design flaws, such as the way that every state in the United States, whether it has 38 million or 600,000 residents, gets two and only two U.S. senators, or how the entire 435-member House of Representatives is put up for re-election every two years, the shortest election calendar in the entire world. Others are crimes of omission, like the document's relative silence about voting rights. But the biggest problem is that it is, as a statistician might put it, underspecified. It doesn't adequately describe the powers granted to the Supreme Court it created, or explain what a militia is in the

Second Amendment, or outline what happens if the Senate decides it simply can't be bothered to carry out its constitutional obligations by approving appointments made by the president. It contains no information about how elections should be funded. And the thing is well nigh impossible to amend. Stuck with a legal order concocted a hundred years before the invention of refrigeration, progressives must find workarounds to fix our political order's design flaws. Importantly, those solutions must be constitutional and able to withstand legal challenges to their constitutionality.

In chapter two I will explain how Republicans have, with Machiavellian zeal, exploited the Constitution's silence on key issues and trashed critical normative understandings that keep American politics and government functioning. Beginning with the Gingrich radicals who took over the House in 1994, the modern GOP has been willing to exploit the constitutional order's reliance on informal understandings between political actors—and the absence of those understandings from the Constitution—to sabotage the functioning of Congress, destroy the Obama presidency, and seize vastly more power than the American people would otherwise have granted them. The theft of Merrick Garland's Supreme Court seat by craven Republicans willing to tolerate the rise of Donald Trump to power in exchange for realizing their cynical goals was the ultimate example of how the GOP abuses the clear spirit of the constitutional order for selfish gain. The chapter outlines how Democrats, now that they are in the minority for the foreseeable future, must pay homage to their overlords and use what little power they have to slow down legislation, turn the public against the GOP Congress, and then retake total power in 2018 and 2020.

What they should do with that power is the subject of the remaining chapters. This is not necessarily a policy platform—advice about which health care stance the party should adopt, or how to approach trade and guns and abortion. I do offer some thoughts about policy in the conclusion, but they are not the centerpiece of this book. The remaining chapters instead offer a series of recommendations as to how Democrats can, fairly easily, pass laws eliminating structural disadvantage, for progressives one after another, by fundamentally altering key aspects of our political system that we take for granted but are not, contrary to popular belief, outlined in the Constitution. Most of the following ideas would require only a law to be passed by a Democratic-controlled Congress and then signed by a Democratic president.

Chapter three describes how granting statehood to Washington, D.C. and Puerto Rico—long-suffering territories whose citizens are utterly deprived of voting rights and representation in federal elections—can help rectify the Democrats' structural imbalance in the United States Senate. The chapter also explains how breaking the deep-blue state of California into seven states can finish the job, by finally creating about as many blue-leaning as red-leaning states and delivering lasting power (or at least parity) to Senate Democrats and their allies.

Chapter four argues that the theft of Merrick Garland's seat by Republicans and the deepening intensity of congressional battles over federal judicial appointments should lead the next Democratic administration to pack the Supreme Court, by adding liberal justices until progressives finally have their first majority in a long generation, as well as creating hundreds of new judgeships in the federal judiciary. The Constitution does not stipulate the number of justices either on the Supreme Court or the lower courts, and Democrats should use the threat of court-packing to press for a constitutional amendment to end lifetime tenure in the federal judiciary as well as enacting other reforms that would finally remove destructive, ugly battles over the courts from our political landscape.

In chapter five, I urge progressives to get behind a change in how we elect our representatives to the House, a reform that would not only eliminate the grotesque chicanery of gerrymandering, but also make it possible for smaller parties to finally win a seat at the governing table. I also recommend doubling the size of the House to bring the constituent-to-legislator ratio more in line with what the Founders envisioned.

Finally, in chapter six, I talk about how any serious progressive governing coalition must immediately address our litany of voting problems, from the disenfranchisement of felons to the racist voter-ID laws implemented by cynical Republicans across the country, by passing a comprehensive new voting rights act.

I conclude with some thoughts about the expansive policy agenda that Democrats should pursue simultaneously, how the foregoing recommendations can help make that policy vision a reality, and how individual progressives can work to make it all happen.

You'll notice that throughout this book I talk mostly about Democrats and the strategies that should be pursued by party leaders, elected officials, and individual voters. But this advice isn't just for the declining numbers of Americans who think of themselves as "Democrats" or who are actually members of the party, but rather for everyone who thinks of themselves as belonging to the progressive left in the United States as a whole. This is not a missive in the ongoing war between the different wings or coalitions in the party, and you won't find anything in these pages litigating Bernie versus Hillary or dwelling on the merits of open and closed primaries. Those are important debates, but they are not the subject of this book. On the contrary, my hope here is to call for unity as we combat the structural inequality in our electoral politics, a project that will benefit the left as a whole but also make possible new political parties, coalitions, and policies. For now, the Democratic Party remains the institutional vehicle of the left, and that is why most of the following recommendations are addressed to its leaders and activists. But to be clear, the hope is to usher in a new age of robust, multiparty competition in which the progressive left has more and better options on Election Day.

Step one in bringing this vision to fruition is to stop bringing pistols to the nuclear war. For Democrats, the purpose of the following noble partisanship is nothing short of dragging the United States kicking and screaming into the twenty-first century, a place where every other advanced capitalist democracy on Earth has realized that you cannot reduce the modern state to its preindustrial shell without killing or immiserating millions of your fellow citizens and that the challenges of modernity require a well-funded, comprehensive national government to mitigate the excesses of global capitalism and to bring about some degree of social justice. To get there, Democrats must be prepared to mimic their tormentors by intentionally destroying the Trump administration and then unleashing this dizzying array of electoral and institutional reforms when they recapture total power.

This book is the blueprint.

Hold my Shiraz.

# IT'S TIME TO FIGHT DIRTY

★ ★ ★ ★

# 1

## The 230-Year Old Airplane

A few blocks from the glittering Constitution Center in Philadelphia is America's oldest continuously inhabited street, Elfreth's Alley. The houses are tiny and cramped, because people were significantly shorter in the eighteenth century,[20] and because the Framers and their friends generally did not believe that you needed to invent new names for extraneous spaces in your homes—there are no great rooms on Elfreth's Alley and no bathrooms large enough to host an intimate dinner party. People actually live in some of these houses, but no contemporary real estate company would ever design such dwellings.

The American Constitution is the Elfreth's Alley of global governance documents, a text that should be seen and admired by tourists, appreciated by historians, and lauded for its contribution to the progress of human liberty. What it should not be, however, is precisely what it currently is: the immobile operating system for an advanced, postindustrial democratic society in the year 2018. This archaic document systematically disadvantages progressives in national elections, both by design and by accident; the American Constitution is a teardown. Unfortunately, like a building that has been designated as a historical landmark by the municipal government, we can't tear down the Constitution. The Framers, with a combination of diabolique and ingenuity, made it almost impossible to amend. Other countries, when faced with serious political, social, or economic problems, are generally able to adapt their constitutions to suit changing times. In America, we are still arguing over the meaning of sentences drafted over candlelight by slaveholders nearly one hundred years before Darwin posited the theory of evolution.

The U.S. Constitution is tremendously lucky to have in its corner a group of cheerless fanatics who believe that our laws must conform to the literal text of the Constitution with no allowance made for changing times, developments in human society, or the objective needs of the present. This doctrine, which was rightly considered completely insane by legal scholars and practitioners within living memory, is known as originalism, and in any other (say, religious) context its adherents would with some justification be referred to as fundamentalists or zealots. The late Antonin Scalia argued that the Constitution should mean what it meant in 1787, or when it was amended. As he argued, "It means today not what current society, much less the court, thinks it ought to mean, but what it meant when it was adopted."[21] In other words, the will of the people, as enshrined in a document drafted more than two centuries ago, will always override the will of the people today. As University of Chicago law professor William Baude puts it, originalists believe "that the words in the Constitution have the same meaning over time, even if modern circumstances change, and even if we wish the words meant something else."[22] For Scalia, those meanings are to be derived from the words in the text as they were understood at the time, rather than what we can glean about the authors' intent from other sources. Other originalists do care what the Framers actually intended when they drafted the Constitution.[23]

The success of originalism can be traced to an ingenious movement launched by judicial radicals in the 1980s, who wanted to build a counterhegemonic movement to fight prevailing liberal interpretations of constitutional jurisprudence as embodied by the many decisions of the Warren Court, including *Roe v. Wade*. Recognizing that conservative political victories since 1968 had not been sufficient to transform the courts, conservative legal scholars, donors, and activists built a movement to compete with liberals on the level of law schools, professional networking, and judicial appointments. As Johns Hopkins University political scientist Steve Teles notes, what they realized was that "ideas need networks through which they can be shared and nurtured, organizations to connect them to problems and to diffuse them to political actors, and patrons to provide resources for these supporting conditions."[24] They built these networks by pursuing an "indirect approach"[25] that involved the creation of the hard-right Federalist Society, a group that started out as a conference at the University of Chicago but has morphed into a lavishly funded group of originalists from which nearly all Republican judicial appointments since George W. Bush have been drawn. By contesting liberal legal theories in "the professions and universities where many of the key resources for elite political change are rooted," Federalist Society legal entrepreneurs were able to increase the visibility and hence the legitimacy of their ideas.[26] What was once shocking and unthinkable—that contemporary problem-solving should be totally subsumed to the literal interpretation of the Constitution—gradually became mainstream conservative judicial philosophy when members of the Federalist Society graduated from law school and made their way into important positions of power in the academy, the legal world, and the federal and state judiciaries.

The Federalist Society and its allies did indeed succeed in building a formidable philosophical movement, linked to conservative activist networks, designed to execute a slow-motion takeover of the federal judiciary. That project stands on the brink of total success—as soon as a Republican president is able to replace either Anthony Kennedy or one of the Supreme Court's liberal justices, they will have their first originalist Supreme Court majority, and their dreams of rolling back the administrative state and returning America to an imagined pre–New Deal utopia will finally come true. At heart, "originalism" as a doctrine is used as a convenient smokescreen to pursue a highly conservative interpretation of the Constitution. Perhaps the most egregious example is the Second Amendment, which has been interpreted by the Roberts Court to mean an unlimited right for private citizens to carry arms. This interpretation makes no sense when looking at the literal words of the text, which contain no such provision, nor by the intent of the Framers, who explicitly rejected an individual-rights model of firearms, which was available to them in certain state constitutions, including Pennsylvania's.[27] By creating a new right (an individual right to bear arms) that is plainly not supported by the text of the Constitution or the debates that surrounded the issue at the time, originalists engaged in the very behavior—judicial activism—that they claim to abhor, by overturning the clear will of the public as expressed through state and municipal legislation. When, for instance, the Roberts Court invalidated Washington, D.C.'s prohibition on firearms, the justices were engaging in the very "legislating from the bench" that they so objected to during the Warren Court.

To make matters worse, originalists are often unwilling to head down the staircase and into the basement where their own doctrine leads them. For instance, the Framers clearly did not intend for their descendants to have the right to walk into the town square carrying their own personal semiautomatic machine guns capable of gunning down an entire British regiment in three minutes. They surely did not intend for their free speech protections to be used as justification for hollow-hearted billionaires to dump millions of dollars into unwatchable campaign attack ads designed by the five worst human beings in every graduating class. But according to the acolytes of this particular school of the jurisprudence, the Constitution is, in the words of Antonin Scalia, "not a living document. It's dead, dead, dead."[28] Nothing matters other than the narrow meaning of the document's words, even if it means saddling the United States with a series of medieval problems that other societies have easily dispensed with.

Strict adherence to the literal text of the Constitution causes contemporary America all manner of needless problems and crises, from the depressing regularity of mass shootings to the unavailability of abortion for so many American women, who have seen the Court gut the spirit of *Roe v. Wade* over time. But the Constitution also created a total mess of a political system. If that mess was equally problematic for Republicans and Democrats, you would probably not be holding this book in your hands. But almost all of the design flaws in U.S. politics today empower Republicans at the expense of Democrats. The most egregious of these affronts to the spirit of democratic rule is the structure of the United States Senate, surely the most malapportioned legislative body on the face of Earth. Home at any given time to dozens of semi-fossilized windbags yammering on about the sacrosanct nature of inane procedures like the filibuster and "senatorial courtesy," the Senate gives each state two and only two Senators. This is how you end up having to shake down even the most sparsely populated of American states for two human beings capable of performing the kind of political work necessary to keep a modern country of 320 million people functioning properly. As in an extremely deep fantasy baseball league, you sometimes need to reach very far for talent, which is the only possible explanation for how someone like Republican Senator Mike Rounds of South Dakota has a job at the highest levels of government in the most powerful country in the history of the planet. Most Americans wouldn't be able to pick this guy out of a lineup of two people, with good reason.

However, we've got bigger issues than the elevation of same-looking mediocrities from nowheresville to the highest offices in the land. The graver problem is that the way the American experiment unfolded over the last two hundred and fifty years created a series of states with tiny populations that have the same right to representation in the Senate—and thus effective veto power over the public policy direction of the country—as the 38 million citizens of California. You can't lay too much blame at the feet of the Framers. At the time California was the property of the Spanish Empire. The small states at the Constitutional Convention—Delaware and Rhode Island are the real villains in this story—refused to commit to the new union unless the larger states agreed to give them equal representation in perpetuity. As the eminent political scientist Robert Dahl argued in *How Democratic Is the American Constitution?* "The solution of equal representation was not, then, a product of constitutional theory, high principle, or grand design. It was nothing more than a practical outcome of a hard bargain that its opponents finally agreed to in order to achieve a constitution."[29]

This completely absurd distortion of democratic principles is often comically rationalized by constitutional pedants as part of some well-thought-out scheme to insure the safety and balance of our democratic experiment. But this is nonsense. The Senate's structure was the result of a lousy compromise. There is no other legislative body on the face of Earth in possession of both the Senate's sweeping powers over American public policy as well as its comical lack of democratic balance. The largest population imbalances between the states in 1787 are tiny in comparison to today's numbers.

The problem is getting worse, rather than better, over time, as large states are growing more quickly than the small states. As political scientist Jeffrey Ladewig and attorney Mathew Jasinski argued in 2003, "while the populations of small states have grown, their relative populations have decreased, which has increased the number of relatively small states."[30] In other words, the degree to which the average Californian or Texan is disadvantaged in the Senate relative to the average Rhode Islander or North Dakotan has grown over time. Residents of the larger states may or may not quite understand how the current electoral system deprives them of influence. Most of the largest U.S. states—chiefly California, New York, Illinois, and Texas—haven't been competitive at the presidential level in a generation, meaning in addition to having almost no power in the U.S. Senate, voters in these states are also completely ignored in presidential election years thanks to another monstrosity bequeathed to us by the Framers, the Electoral College. This profoundly undemocratic institution has gifted the presidency to a Republican runner-up twice this century and remains one of the hardest things about American politics to explain to outsiders who naturally expect that the winner of a national election for a single office to be the person with the most votes. As Dahl, one of the Constitution's most insightful critics, argued about the Electoral College, "Probably nothing the Framers did illustrates more sharply their inability to foresee the shape that politics would assume in a democratic republic."[31]

The Constitution is also obscenely difficult to amend. The procedures that the Constitution's architects put into place to alter our country's charter are the legal equivalent of an advancing army blowing up a bridge behind it. Changing the Constitution requires a two-thirds majority in both chambers of Congress, something that now generally happens only to name monuments and declare uncontroversial national holidays. If that were the only bar to clear, it would still be pretty high, but surmountable. But in addition to the supermajorities in Congress, the Constitution also demands that three-fourths of state legislatures also ratify the amendment. (Curiously, there is no role for the president.) The Constitution has only been amended twenty-seven times in its two hundred and thirty years of existence, and the pace of change has slowed dramatically in modern times. The Constitution has not been amended at all since 1992, when a long-stalled amendment related to congressional salary increases was finally ratified, and it has not been changed at the behest of modern Americans since 1971, when the Twenty-sixth Amendment lowered the voting age from twenty-one to eighteen, partly due to outrage that young people were being sent to fight and die in Vietnam yet could not register their approval or disapproval of national policy.

One way of thinking about how polarization has immobilized the Constitution is that the amendment to change the voting age would never be ratified today, since younger voters now lean so heavily Democratic that Republicans would dismiss such a massive extension of voting rights out of hand. Eighteen- to twenty-four-year-olds voted for Hillary Clinton over Donald Trump by a yawning twenty-two-point margin, and you can rest assured that no Republican in Congress or in state legislatures would agree to any change to our founding document that privileges Democrats, even if it is the right thing to do. This is why the progressive dream of amending the Constitution to overturn the Citizens United Supreme Court decision is so farcical—unless Democrats magically find themselves in control of three-quarters of our state governments as well as congressional supermajorities, such an amendment is dead on arrival. Even something as sensible as amending the Constitution to abolish the Electoral College has been and will continue to be dismissed by Republicans simply because they are the beneficiary of this inequity. The only way we would reach a national consensus on the Electoral College would be if a Democrat won the presidency despite losing the popular vote, something that very nearly happened in 2004, when John Kerry came within 100,000 votes of flipping Ohio and thus capturing the presidency despite losing to George W. Bush by more than 3 million votes nationwide.

The near-impossibility of amending the Constitution means Americans are stuck with a series of electoral procedures and national policies that they actively despise. For most of this century, a wide majority of Americans has supported amending the U.S. Constitution to abolish the Electoral College and to choose the winner of presidential elections according to the crazy principle of who wins the most votes.[32] Between 2012 and 2016 that majority narrowed, and in the aftermath of the 2016 election, 47 percent of

Americans supported the Electoral College as is. But it's still underwater. The Republican appointees of George W. Bush and Donald Trump have helped preserve interpretations of the Constitution that are deeply unpopular. For instance, a twenty-one-point majority of Americans supports stricter laws on guns,[33] yet the country is held hostage to its obsolete Second Amendment and the judicial zealots whose interpretation of the Framers' words is more or less settled constitutional law, whereas a dedicated and loud minority of gun fanatics opposes all laws restricting what kind of guns Americans can own and even holds up research into how we might be mass murdered by AR-15–wielding misanthropes somewhat less often.[34] One poll suggested that the Equal Rights Amendment has the support of 94 percent of Americans,[35] yet is going nowhere anytime soon thanks to implacable opposition from conservatives. Antonin Scalia, the chief originalist on the Supreme Court until his sudden death in February 2016, spoke for the conservative position on the ERA when he argued that "Certainly the Constitution does not require discrimination on the basis of sex. The only issue is whether it prohibits it. It doesn't."[36] A significant majority of Americans expresses satisfaction with America's pioneering system of public education, yet students and families watch helplessly as market fundamentalists perform a slow-moving, hostile takeover of the system, while the perfectly reasonable option of writing equal education funding into the Constitution is just off the table. And the structure of the Senate is doubly impossible to change: The Constitution plainly states that "no state, without its consent, shall be deprived of its equal suffrage in the Senate." The small states will obviously never grant that consent, which would diminish their power. Reapportioning the Senate is a nonstarter.

The U.S. Constitution also features, destructively, the most frequent legislative election schedule in the entire world by putting the entire 435-member House of Representatives up for election every two years. Two years probably seemed like a really long time in 1787—it was certainly much longer than most newborns could expect to live prior to the invention of antibiotics. Back then it made some sense to hold such frequent elections given the rate at which congressmen were going pecs up—in the first ten years of the new republic, twelve congressmen died in office (though not necessarily in *an* office).

The Framers certainly could not have foreseen that our national elections would turn into a multibillion dollar, fifty-ring circus that consumes an absurd amount of the time available to our national representatives. House minority leader Nancy Pelosi told NPR in 2012 that she attends about four hundred(!) fundraisers every single year.[37] Former House member Walt Minnick (D-ID) said that he took just five days off from fundraising after winning his seat in the 2008 elections. In 2013, the Huffington Post obtained a PowerPoint presentation prepared by the Democratic Congressional Campaign Committee recommending that new members spend *four hours a day* making fundraising calls.[38] Rep. Rick Nolan (D-MN) claims that both parties encourage their members to spend an astonishing thirty hours a week fundraising, at call centers set up on the Hill for maximum convenience.[39] If elections were less frequent—say, every four years rather than every two—it would somewhat relieve members of Congress of an obligation that (a) they all detest and (b) prevents them from doing the people's business with their working hours. It seems implausible that the American people, who in general are not especially diligent or enthusiastic about voting in the first place, would mind being consulted less often about their House representatives. But, alas, there it is in plain, incontestable language in Article 1, Section 2: "The House of Representatives shall be composed of Members chosen every second Year by the People of the several States." So here we are, two hundred and thirty years later, scrambling for elections what seems like every five minutes because of the whims of our long-dead ancestors.

Some of the Constitution's flaws were written into the text but have not held up very well with the passage of time, like lifetime tenure in the federal court system. Others, however, are crimes of omission, like the document's silence about voting. As Garrett Epps argued, "The right to vote of citizens of the United States remains a kind of stepchild in the family of American rights, perhaps because it is not listed in the Bill of Rights, and perhaps because Americans still retain the Framers' ambivalence about democracy."[40] There are perfectly understandable reasons why the Constitution offers relatively slim guidance about voting. At the time of the founding, there was not a single functional democracy as we would understand the term today in the entire world, voting by secret ballot existed nowhere, and the authors distrusted ordinary citizens to make wise decisions anyway. The Constitution's architects, of course, infamously left voting rights to the states, most of which restricted the franchise to white, male property owners. And they would have regarded the subsequent expansions of voting rights in the United States with considerable horror. The Constitution also contains no guidance about how to conduct elections to the House of Representatives. In fact, until the mid-nineteenth century, many congressional districts in the United States had multiple winners, a fact that has been lost to history. The entire architecture of American elections, from the size of the districts to the complex system of party primaries, was created long after the Constitution was written and would be shockingly easy to change.

The most glaring and problematic omission from the Constitution is its silence about how to resolve disagreements between the executive and legislative branches of government. The direct election of a president, separate from the legislature, is one of the key distinctions between our presidential system of government and parliamentary democracies. In parliamentary systems, the prime minister is an elected member of parliament and nearly always the leader of the party with the most seats. As the political scientist Juan Linz once put it, parliament is "the only democratically legitimate institution."[41] You can't have "divided government" in a place like the United Kingdom. You can have an election where no party gets a majority and must govern in conjunction with other groups. But you cannot have a situation where one party is given the right to draft the laws and another party has the right to sign and carry them out. The fact that the clash between the executive and legislative branches has never resulted in the breakdown of democracy in the United States[42] is more luck than design. In Linz's words, "The American system works or has worked in spite of, rather than because of, the presidential constitution of the United States."[43]

In "The Perils of Presidentialism," one of the most famous standalone articles ever written in the field of political science, Linz says that the creation of two competing centers of power and legitimacy is one of the most combustible features of presidential democracies and one of the main reasons that so many countries that use versions of American democracy have collapsed repeatedly into authoritarianism. Holding legislative elections in the middle of the executive's term only makes matters worse—voters have nearly always empowered the opposition party in those elections, but because the legal order leaves the president in place, even if he is deeply unpopular, it just exacerbates the problem. In that sense, American politics probably would have been more functional had Republicans toppled President Obama in 2010 or 2014 (or had Democrats been able to dislodge George W. Bush from power in 2006). Instead, voters were delivered the worst of both worlds because both Obama and his congressional adversaries believed they had been granted a mandate to pursue their irreconcilable visions of public policy.

To be sure, this arrangement has its defenders. "Checks and balances" seems to be one of the few governance concepts successfully taught to high school students in this country. Political scientist David Mayhew has long argued that divided government actually works pretty well. "Divided party control is not a problem," he claimed in a 2009 article[44] that cited the productivity of the 110th

Congress, which was controlled by Democrats but passed a significant amount of legislation signed by Republican President George W. Bush. Mayhew made this argument, at book length, about the entire postwar period from 1946 to 2002. Divided government may increase dysfunction, he claimed, but "important laws have materialized at a rate largely unrelated to conditions of party control."[45] However, Mayhew's investigation, and his conclusions, are drawn from a particularly unusual period of party comity in U.S. national history, in which there was substantially more overlap in ideology than there was, for example, when pro-slavery Democrats controlled Congress in the early 1850s and the last Whig president, Millard Fillmore, ground policymaking to a halt. The Thirty-second Congress (1851–1853) was one of the least productive in the history of the Republic, passing only seventy-four bills that were ultimately signed by the president.[46] We all know where that led. One could argue that the issues facing us today are similarly grave, and the differences between parties just as unbridgeable.

Unfortunately, directly addressing the Constitution's shortfalls in the current political climate is not feasible. A constitutional convention can technically be called when two-thirds of the states express their desire for one, but such a path poses incredible risks for everyone involved. Although there is actually a little-known and little-talked-about movement gaining steam to do exactly that—mostly from red-state legislatures wanting to amend the Constitution to pass a balanced budget amendment, and from progressives disillusioned with the Citizens United decision—once a convention is called, then the entire constitutional order could theoretically be rewritten.[47] And one thing is for sure: if that convention were to happen today, we would be in for an even more conservative constitutional regime than the one we already have, because conservatives are in control of so many state legislatures.

This is why a new constitutional convention has also become a kind of pet project of the extreme right, with notable proponents like the American Legislative Exchange Council (ALEC), Texas Governor Greg Abbott, and Florida U.S. Senator Marco Rubio. If Republican extremists were somehow to control the balance of power in such proceedings, the results would be extraordinarily ugly, with a new legal order that diminishes the ability of the federal government to spend money addressing national problems. Indeed, were such a convention actually on the horizon, it could raise the stakes of national politics to unbearable and possibly disastrous and violent levels. The Constitution is also sufficiently vague on the subject of this convention that it would inspire all kinds of problematic jockeying and disagreement—how are delegates to that convention elected? Does Congress need to ratify any amendments made? How would the public react to their representatives calling a convention even though no one has campaigned on it or even told the voters that this was coming?

All of this means that if progressive leaders are going to craft workarounds to some of the problems of contemporary American politics, they are going to have to do so within the framework of the U.S. Constitution rather than outside of it.

To do this, Democrats and their allies are going to have to hold the line for the remainder of Trump's term in office. Remaining unified as a party to obstruct and thwart as much of the GOP agenda as possible will help make the GOP brand even more toxic than it already is. And if and when Democrats recapture state and national power in 2018 and 2020, they must design clever workarounds to the Constitution's flaws, and rectify the institutional power imbalance that currently favors the GOP and promises to do so indefinitely absent a massive and sudden shift in the political, economic, and social values of rural Americans. Activists and partisans must, for now, give up the dream of amending the U.S. Constitution. Instead, they should urge their leaders to use the powers that they actually have, to increase the number of states in the union, change the way the House is elected and increase its size, add additional justices to the Supreme Court, and enact sweeping changes in how we vote and who is allowed to do so. These changes, none of which require constitutional amendments, should allow Democrats and their allies, including newly empowered third and fourth parties that will caucus with Democrats, to finally break the gridlock that has characterized national policymaking since the 1990s and to transform the United States into a functional modern social democracy that, for the very first time in history, successfully delivers a bare minimum of security, opportunity, and genuine equality to all of its citizens. These changes will not eliminate each of the Constitution's premodern features or resolve all of the tensions that the document created, but they will bring the United States much closer to the evolving practices of other democratic societies, and most importantly, they will overcome the Constitution's systematic bias against the contemporary Democratic coalition.

First, though, they need to get themselves back into power.

Here's how.

★ 2 ★

# I Learned It by Watching You: The New Procedural Warfare

Three weeks after Donald Trump's shocking "victory" over Hillary Clinton in the 2016 presidential election, strategists Kellyanne Conway and Jennifer Palmieri squared off at a Harvard roundtable that dissected the twists and turns of the contest. A visibly angry Palmieri looked at Conway and stated, "I would rather lose than win the way you guys did."[48] On the one hand, Palmieri's declaration was an admirable statement of support for bare-minimum standards of decency and fair play even in hotly contested elections. Democrats should certainly not be willing, as Team Trump was, to play footsie with the very worst elements of their coalition. On the other hand, allow me to politely dissent: Democrats could stand to get just a bit dirtier in their politics. Indeed, they will not come back to power by acting like Democrats—pragmatic public servants willing to compromise with their adversaries across the aisle to get important public policies implemented. They must, instead, fight as ruthlessly as they possibly can.

As political scientist David Karpf wrote in the immediate aftermath of Black Tuesday, "Representative Democracy operates on the basis of formal laws and informal norms. The laws (particularly the constitution) dictate what people *must* do. The norms dictate what people *ought* to do."[49] In recent years, the American constitutional order has proven to be tremendously vulnerable to the erosion of important norms that keep the government functioning as designed. The most important of these norms is the expectation that when different branches of government are controlled by different political parties, they will compromise and work together for the greater good. For most of the country's modern history, a broadly shared informal understanding between the parties mostly spared the country ugly fights over Supreme Court nominations: the president has the right to nominate more or less whoever he or she wants, within reason, so long as the proposed jurist has the requisite qualifications and is not obviously a hack. (The latter requirement, for instance, scuttled George W. Bush's nomination of Harriet Miers.) This right holds even when the opposition party controls the Senate. Or it did. The Merrick Garland fiasco exposed the weakness of the Constitution's normative underpinnings when Republicans decided they simply would not allow Barack Obama to fill the seat of Antonin Scalia, a cutthroat procedural move that paid off when Donald Trump unexpectedly won the 2016 presidential election and therefore the right to fill Scalia's seat with the chiseled originalist Neil Gorsuch.

The Merrick Garland imbroglio was not, however, an aberration but rather the culmination of eight years of ruthless and destructive political warfare that saw the Republicans grind national governance in the United States to a standstill using what Mark Tushnet has called "constitutional hardball."[50] For much of the post-World War II period in American politics, bipartisanship was the norm rather than the exception. While the parties might disagree sharply on public policy, presidents could get legislation passed even when the opposition controlled Congress. As the late Democrat Tip O'Neill—who was the Speaker of the House during the Reagan Administration and used to chat regularly and amiably with the Gipper and his Republican counterparts—put it, "That, to me, is the special greatness of our political system. There's no rancor or hatred—only the energetic clash of conflicting ideas."[51] The contemporary Republican Party took that clash of ideas and turned it into a clash of legitimacy and a crisis of American democracy. As the minority party from 2009 to 2011 they did this by slowing down legislation in the House and Senate and using the filibuster to harass and delay even routine pieces of legislation and uncontroversial nominations. Then once they captured the House of Representatives in the 2010 midterms, they decided that the best way to complete their conquest of Washington would be to turn the chamber into a legislative graveyard where new policy is buried but never, ever made. Then-Senate Minority Leader Mitch McConnell did not even bother trying to hide what they were doing, infamously proclaiming that his most important goal was to "make Barack Obama a one-term president." In his victory speech the night he inflicted a double-digit defeat on Democratic challenger Alison Lundergan Grimes in November 2014, McConnell took to the podium and promised a bipartisanship that he has not spent one second pursuing: "We do have an obligation to work together on issues where we can agree," he said. "I think we have a duty to do that. Just because we have a two party system doesn't mean we have to be in perpetual conflict."

The cynicism was positively breathtaking. Earlier in the speech, he said, "Whether you're a coal miner in Eastern Kentucky who can't find work or a mom in Paducah who doesn't understand why the government just took away her family's health insurance, I've heard your concerns."[52] The government, of course, hadn't taken anyone's health care away—as we would discover in 2017, it was McConnell and his allies who planned to snatch health insurance from poor folks in rural Kentucky by eliminating the Affordable Care Act's Medicaid expansion. It would be their own senator who would do the dirty work of trying to shepherd the repeal through Congress and thus deprive hundreds of thousands of down-on-their-luck Kentuckians of their access to the health care system in one of the country's poorest states. The victorious senator had, of course, spent years trying to undo Obama's achievement of executing the single greatest expansion of access to health insurance in American history. Other than reducing federal spending, congressional Republicans could not claim a single policy achievement since 2006.

There is some revisionist history floating around the ether these days that Democrats share an equal amount of the blame for the total breakdown in interparty relations. This is bananas. The destruction of American governing norms was a one-party show featuring an endless, nihilistic monologue by the Republicans. Even before they retook the House, the Republican Party had become, in the sharp and prophetic words of Norm Ornstein and Thomas Mann, an "insurgent outlier—ideologically extreme; contemptuous of the inherited social and economic policy regime; scornful of compromise; unpersuaded by conventional understanding of facts, evidence, and science; and dismissive of the legitimacy of its political opposition."[53] McConnell and the Republicans pointedly refused to compromise with President Obama, even when the fiscal health of the Republic was at stake, and even when Obama was dangling long-sought policy concessions to the political right, including scaling back Social Security benefits and balancing the budget for the long term. They struck this obstructionist pose from the very first day that Obama took office. Republican obstruction in the Senate had gotten so far out of hand by 2013 that Majority Leader Harry Reid made the decision to abolish the filibuster for lower-court nominees and cabinet officials. By some measures, Republicans blocked more judicial nominees between 2009 and 2013 than had ever been blocked in the entire history of the United States. Republicans in 2013 were sitting on all nominees to the D.C. Court of Appeals, arguing preposterously that the Court was "underworked" and in need of shrinkage. After they assumed control of the Senate in January of 2015, Republicans confirmed just two appellate court justices for the remainder of Barack Obama's term.

Another way to understand how Democrats need to get better at manipulating the loopholes in the constitutional order is to look at the use of the filibuster in the U.S. Senate. The filibuster is another one of those curious American democratic institutions, found nowhere else on the planet, that citizens take more or less for granted. Senate rules allow unlimited debate on any piece of legislation as long as a senator can hold the floor without yielding, unless a certain number of votes can be mustered to close debate—a process known as a "cloture" vote. Sixty is the number of votes needed to "invoke cloture" and close debate. The filibuster is, of course, nowhere to be found in the U.S. Constitution, and is in fact merely an artifact of the rules of the chamber, something that could be eliminated in a matter of minutes if the majority party so desired. Under its modern incarnation, it forces legislators to put together sixty votes in the one hundred-person Senate to get virtually anything done. In the public imagination, the filibuster is a popular, colorful tactic used by skilled orators to hold up proceedings on some important piece of legislation about which they have major philosophical objections. Think Jimmy Stewart in *Mr. Smith Goes To Washington* announcing that "I've got a few things I'd like to say to this body," before launching into a long diatribe against the corporate malfeasance holding up efforts to relieve suffering during the Great Depression. "The people of my State," Stewart's senator thundered, "need permanent relief from the crooks riding their backs."[54]

More often, of course, it has been used by opponents of social progress to obstruct, as white supremacists in the Senate did for years, typified by Strom Thurmond's twenty-four hour, eighteen-minute filibuster of the Civil Rights Act in 1957, which he prepared for by deliberately dehydrating himself so he wouldn't have to take a bathroom break.[55] But the way it is used today, in fact, means that the back-riding crooks are the obstructionists in the U.S. Senate who will stop at nothing to prevent duly constituted majorities from acting in the public interest. As David Mayhew notes, this hyper-obstructionism was not at all how Congress functioned before the modern era, when filibusters were much more rare. "Across a wide range of issues," he argues, "I doubt that the Senate of the past had any anti-majoritarian barrier as concrete, as decisive, or as consequential as today's rule of 60."[56]

If that's all it were, it would be bad enough. But the filibuster as a tactic has been distorted beyond recognition. Today, hardly anyone is forced to actually hold the Senate floor and justify their decision to slow down or halt proceedings on legislation in the Senate. Because much of the noncontroversial business of the Senate is conducted via something called a Unanimous Consent Agreement (UCA), all Senators need to do is to notify the majority leader of their intent to withhold unanimous consent, more commonly known as placing a "hold." Think of a "hold" as signifying the senator's *intent* to filibuster. On the floor, any one senator can force the majority leader to hold a vote on a "motion to proceed." Such votes are also subject to a cloture vote, and cloture votes require hours of debate.

Ultimately, if the majority leader doesn't have sixty votes, there is no need for senators who object to the bill to hold the floor and read *Goodnight Moon* over and over again for twenty-three hours straight. (More on how Democrats could change this follows.) As Nicholas O. Howard and Jason M. Roberts put it, "Senators signal their intent to object to a UCA—in essence a threat to filibuster—by sending a letter to their party leader indicating that he or she will or may object to a unanimous consent request on a particular measure."[57] To make matters even worse, holds are kept private unless they are announced by the initiator on the Senate floor, meaning the public has no idea who is even holding up the legislation unless the person obstructing cops to it publicly. The process has become so byzantine that the Congressional Research Service has identified six different types of holds, including the colorfully named "Mae West hold," designed "to foster negotiation and bargaining between proponents and opponents."[58]

Over time, holds have been used by the minority party to hold up legislation that has made it out of committee and which the majority leader intends to bring to the Senate floor. The intent is not murky:

holds are usually designed to strangle bills in their sleep. Without the holding senator being forced to take the floor and explain his or her rationale, it simply looks to the public like the Senate can't get a damn thing done. This is particularly hard for citizens to understand when one party controls Congress and the presidency. Why, they must wonder, can't the government get anything done *even now*? Why did we send these clowns to Washington, anyway? The use of holds can wax and wane in predictable ways, but they were rampant during the Obama Administration between 2009 and 2015, when Democrats held the majority in the Senate and Republicans used the tactic to stall or kill any legislation that the majority party wanted to pursue. Republicans were particularly ruthless after they took over the Senate majority in 2014. Senator Tom Cotton (R-AR), for instance, objected to a slew of Obama foreign policy nominees just to slow the process down, and McConnell ultimately didn't bring them up for a vote.

The butcher's bill for six years of this kind of obstruction was enormous. It is no exaggeration to say that between January 2011, when the GOP assumed control of the U.S. House of Representatives, and January 2017, when Donald Trump and his Vichy Republicans took over all three branches of the American government, no national problems were addressed, let alone resolved. The 112th, 113th, and 114th Congresses were among the least productive legislative assemblies in the history of this or any republic. Instead of working with Democrats to fix some of the problems with the Affordable Care Act in the public interest, Republicans in the House voted more than fifty times to repeal it without offering their own alternative, despite knowing that their futile gesture would immediately be vetoed by President Obama. They used attacks on the ACA as poison pills attached to other pieces of legislation. They shut down the U.S. federal government in an attempt to force President Obama to make key concessions on his party's signature legislative achievement. They engaged in dangerous brinkmanship with the debt ceiling, imperiling America's credit and threatening to plunge the country into an economic catastrophe.

They knew—every last one of them, from John Boehner and Paul Ryan down to the lowliest foot soldier in the movement conservative army—that they had no chance to actually destroy the ACA while Obama was still in office. Nevertheless, they persisted, creating an ugly spectacle of dysfunction so comprehensive that it drove voter turnout in the 2014 midterms down to a new post-World War II low. The atmosphere in D.C. became so poisonous that political scientists started churning out analyses of partisan polarization and how to overcome it, while otherwise levelheaded observers began to see in our politics the makings of a massive constitutional crisis. In October 2015, *Vox* writer Matthew Yglesias wrote an influential essay called "American Democracy is Doomed." Surveying the torched landscape of partisan warfare and state dysfunction since the Gingrich Republicans swept to power in the House in 1994, he predicted that our constitutional order was on a glide path to total destruction. He wrote that American politics was "unsustainably lurching from crisis to crisis" and that, ultimately, the United States might be forced to pursue a new constitutional order in the wake of a total collapse of the state's legitimacy and underlying functionality.[59] Dylan Matthews, also writing for *Vox*, argued that the American government was a "nightmare." Unlike Yglesias, he didn't foresee a collapse of the constitutional order and its replacement by something better, modeled on other, more functional democracies, but rather the rise of the presidency as what he called "an elective dictatorship."[60]

Both writers were referring to a development known in political science as "democratic backsliding"—the process of democratic systems gradually becoming less inclusive and democratic rather than disappearing in the gunpowder explosions of a coup, as most citizens probably imagine that democracies tend to die. The coup model, which is what happened when, for instance, the Chilean government of Salvador Allende was erased by the military seizure of power led by General Augusto Pinochet, is actually a rare occurrence. More frequently, democracies "die in darkness," as the now famous masthead motto of the post-Trump *Washington Post* argues.

Indeed, after the election of Trump, both journalists and increasingly political scientists saw another step in the breakdown of American democracy. Robert Mickey, Steven Levistky, and Lucan Ahmad Way argued that despite public confidence in the integrity of democracy, the United States is not at all immune from the kinds of forces that have scuttled democratic experiments in other societies. "As polarization increases," they argued, "Congress passes fewer and fewer laws and leaves important issues unresolved. Such dysfunction has eroded public trust in political institutions, and along partisan lines."[61]

To understand why Democrats can no longer play the role of pragmatic, nonideological brokers in Congress, you have to understand what has happened to the broader political system since the election of Ronald Reagan in 1980. Political scientists increasingly see polarization as a major structural problem. While scholars are split about how polarized citizens are, there is no question that ordinary people have adopted distinct positions on major issues and have migrated toward the "correct" party that represents their feelings. As Marc J. Hetherington and Jonathan D. Weiler argued in a prominent 2009 book, "Polarization of elites has not led to a polarization of opinion among mass partisans, at least in the strict definitional understanding of the word. Instead, these ordinary people have sorted themselves better into the correct party given their existing ideological proclivities."[62] Disturbing numbers of Americans regard members of the opposing party not just political adversaries, but "as a threat to the nation's well-being."[63] In 2016, 60 percent of Democrats and 63 percent of Republicans wanted their children to marry someone from the same party.[64] Events since the election of Donald Trump have only confirmed that citizens are both sorting themselves into competing camps and taking their cues from party elites about what they should believe. You can see this in the instant transformation of popular GOP opinion about Russian President Vladimir Putin, which jumped twenty points in a single electoral cycle.[65] Trump signaled to voters that Russia is OK, and the voters followed suit. GOP voters are now likely to express approval for things like court-ordered shutterings of news organizations that are "biased." After Trump's disgusting equivocation about the neo-Nazi violence in Charlottesville, Virginia in August 2017, Republican voters told one pollster that they would prefer Jefferson Davis over Barack Obama as president by 25 points.[66]

Moreover, the findings of political scientists on the underlying causes of our dysfunction began to gain some media traction. Kenneth Poole, Howard Rosenthal, and more recent collaborators have, since the 1980s, maintained a database of ideology in the U.S. Congress that assigns each member a complex score on two dimensions of the traditional left-right political spectrum—social and economic issues. Conservative political observer Sean Trende of *RealClearPolitics* called this data "one of the great achievements of modern political science."[67] The findings of this data are pretty unambiguous. Since the early 1980s, Democrats in Congress have become marginally more liberal, but the change, at least as of 2014, was not especially remarkable. On the other hand, during this same time period, the Republican Party has more or less marched off the ideological map. In the long, post-WWII era, it was common for some of the most liberal members of the Republican Party to be more ideologically progressive than the most conservative members of the Democratic Party, and vice versa.[68]

Although some of this overlap was not borne of good intentions or high public spirit—much of it was attributable to the existence of racist white Democrats in the U.S. South—the relative closeness of the two parties made it possible for the country to be governed even when one party did not control all the levers of power. It meant that the two most important post-WWII Republicans prior to Ronald Reagan—Dwight Eisenhower and Richard Nixon—pursued some policies that we would now associate with the Democrats, such as the creation of the Environmental Protection Agency (EPA), the process of engaging with the Chinese regime and the negotiation of nuclear arms reduction treaties with the Soviet Union. That bipartisan comity is deader than Richard Nixon. Republicans found the loopholes in the American constitution and successfully wrecked most of Barack Obama's last six years in office. This created a bizarre and one-sided political dynamic—as Republicans increasingly acted like a unified parliamentary bloc and voted to please their most extreme partisans in the primary electorate, Democrats continued to waste time seeking reasonable compromise with implacable adversaries who had no intention of identifying middle ground, let alone occupying it. Before the current era of polarization, a party would almost certainly have been sent packing for so obviously placing its political interests above the thoughtful pursuit of political compromise. Republicans, instead, found themselves gaining power at all levels during the Obama era because their unified, unbreakable obstruction made the party in power look hapless.

Again, none of this chicanery was illegal according to the Constitution. Indeed, the dark genius of the Obama-era Republicans was precisely in finding the stress points in an underspecified constitutional order, and ruthlessly exploiting them. This is how they refused to confirm Obama's nomination of future Senator Elizabeth Warren to lead the newly created Consumer Protection Bureau and why they held up the eventual agency head for as long as they possibly could. Republicans realized that they could actually cripple the functioning of federal agencies they wanted to abolish simply by slow-rolling the president's nominees. It was designed to make Obama and the Democrats look weak and ineffectual, and to draw the maximum possible contrast between the governing party and the opposition. As Mann and Ornstein note, this was the strategy pioneered by Newt Gingrich in the late 1980s and early 1990s—stop helping a president from the opponent's party govern, and like magic, that president's popularity will take a dive. "The core strategy was to destroy the institution in order to save it, to so intensify public hatred of Congress that voters would buy into the notion of the need for sweeping change and throw the majority bums out."[69] And in that, their Machiavellian strategy succeeded beyond their wildest fantasies.

Throughout the Obama Era, Democrats clung to the hope that voters would punish the Republican Party for its obstructionism. This was the hope when Republicans used catastrophic brinksmanship to shut down the federal government in the fall of 2013, costing taxpayers tens of millions of dollars. This was the hope when Mitch McConnell and his allies decided they would just hold a Supreme Court seat open instead of confirming Barack Obama's nominee. Voters were disgusted. The approval rating of Congress was on par with Stalin or head lice. Decisive majorities favored allowing Obama to forward a nominee to the Supreme Court. Instead, the GOP won sweeping victories in 2010 and 2014, and put the cherry on top by consolidating control over the House, the Senate, and the presidency in 2016. It is hard to avoid a depressing but important realization: the American people just don't care that much about the inside-baseball machinations of D.C. politicos. The procedural gimmicks of parliamentary procedure are almost completely unknown and badly understood even by those who think they know how a bill becomes law or what happens to legislation in committee. Only a tiny fraction of voters could explain what cloture is or how a filibuster works or what the Constitution even says about the Senate's obligation to consider presidential nominees.

If elites are polarized, and ordinary citizens are increasingly radicalized and taking their cues from party leadership, there seems to be little point in Democrats spending precious political capital cooperating with their adversaries. Not only will the resulting policy disappoint their own most committed activists, it will also make Trump and his allies look good. For that reason, the best path forward for congressional Democrats under President Trump is to mimic the same kind of ruthless obstructionism that was modeled for them by their tormentors during President Obama's administration. For a brief period after the election, it was not clear that the party would be able to process this lesson, or to act on it. Indeed, the Trump campaign made a lot of noises that suggested it might pursue policies that had the potential to split the Democratic coalition. Had Trump, for instance, pursued his hard-line immigration crackdown while simultaneously nationalizing the health care system or making real public investment in infrastructure, he might have been able to put Democrats in a much more difficult position. Imagine what might have happened had President Trump proposed a gargantuan investment in mass transit, highways, and other aging features of America's infrastructure, paid for with tax dollars and designed to put as many citizens to work as possible. This lose-lose political situation for Democrats would have created an impossible dilemma for Chuck Schumer and Nancy Pelosi—rally support for good policy, and you make the president look competent and bipartisan, thereby decreasing your own chances of retaking power. Oppose the infrastructure investment and you score political points at the expense of achieving a long-sought progressive policy goal. Republicans throughout the Obama era repeatedly chose option B, and then rode public dissatisfaction with Washington to total power.

Luckily, Democrats have not had to make this difficult political choice. Within days of his inauguration, it became painfully clear that President Trump either did not believe his own populist rhetoric—during the campaign he repeatedly promised not to touch Medicare or Medicaid and to make sure more people had access to health insurance—or that he was too detached from the details of policies supported by his congressional allies to even understand what was happening. With the selection of each official for his oligarch's sampler cabinet of visigoths and magnates, Trump's determination to align himself with the zealots and fabulists in the House Freedom Caucus became harder to deny. He selected HFC alum Mick Mulvaney to be his budget director. Obamacare hardliner Tom Price (R-GA) was selected to run the Department of Health and (In)Human Services. Climate lunatic Scott Pruitt was tapped for the Environmental Protection Agency. Education privatization hardliner Betsy DeVos—who boasted no qualifications for the position other than donating her inherited wealth to rent-seekers and vulture capitalists interested in strip mining the public education system—was nominated to lead the Education Department. When the picks weren't ideologues, they were patently unqualified goons, like the walking narcolepsy public awareness campaign named Ben Carson who is now disinterestedly running the Housing and Urban Development, and the somnambulant ExxonMobil CEO Rex Tillerson as the leader of America's diplomatic efforts at State.

Taken together, these choices indicated a comprehensive and shocking betrayal of the voters who had put Trump into office—the vaunted White Working Class, whose pulse was taken in the months following the election more often than a patient in cardiac arrest in stories so similar ("In a Youngstown diner, long-haul trucker Roger Thompson told us that he has no regrets about the vote he cast for Trump") that they lent themselves to deep satire—one *Deadspin* writer called them "Cletus Safaris." Suddenly, Democrats who had been losing sleep over how to triangulate the unique threat posed by a populist Republican President could now take a much more inflexible stance. Trump was selling out his own voters, not to mention the majority that voted against him. Whether to obstruct was no longer a choice but a decision that had basically been made for them, like *Mad Men*'s Don Draper ordering for you at a restaurant.

The lady will have the partisan warfare, please. And a martini.

★

But the sad truth is that obstruction in the service of noble progressive ideals holds whether the Republicans stand by their man-child, replace him with Vice President Pence—a man known during his time in Congress as Mike Dense—or travel even further down the line of succession to reach House Majority Leader Paul Ryan or the President Pro Tempore of the Senate, Utah's fossilized Orrin Hatch. That is because the GOP is no longer a normal participant in the American two-party system, but rather a dangerous, delegitimizing organization that will eventually bring the United States to a serious constitutional crisis—or worse—if it is not decisively crushed sometime in the near future. And while a lot of colorful words have been tossed at the GOP in the past ten years, it is the discipline of political science that offers the best way to understand what the contemporary Republican Party has turned into.

Little known in America, the late Italian political scientist Giovanni Sartori is still considered to be one of the world's most incisive researchers and analysts of party politics in democratic countries. In the 1970s, he popularized the term "antisystem party" to refer to an agreement that "would not change—if it could—the government but the very system of government."[70] As he put it, an antisystem party "does not share the values of the political order within which it operates."[71] Sartori applied this concept to the far left and far right parties of postwar Europe—communists and fascists and other actors who participated in democratic politics but whose underlying goals were either to destroy it or to replace it with a radically different system (or both). Sartori worried about what he called the "delegitimizing impact" of a party embedded in the political system that constantly calls into question the baseline legitimacy of its opposition. While delegitimizing rhetoric is not limited to the right, it has become unusually acute in far-right media spaces. You can see it in the preelection rhetoric of those who supported President Trump reluctantly—that it would be better to burn down the entire political order than allow Hillary Clinton to win the election.

The Trump Administration has made this problem even worse by delegitimizing the entire mainstream media as well as other sources of expertise, including the Congressional Budget Office, which the President called "fake news."

Sartori also worried about escalation. Because antisystem parties in postwar Europe generally had little chance of actually taking power, they could make outrageous promises—the equivalent of writing checks that will never and can never be cashed. Political scientists now call this process of escalating promises, increasingly unmoored from political, economic or social reality, "outbidding." More than anything else, the GOP in the Obama years resembled one of these organizations, which Sartori argues are designed to act irresponsibly in the political order. Now that Republicans are in power again, they face a challenge that European communists never did: how to actually deliver on their unhinged promises to the public. When you consider that voters generally expect too much of our politics to begin with, the situation seems potentially explosive. Apart from their late-night, half-baked rewrite of America's tax code in December 2017, performed transparently for their donors and met with icy hostility by voters, Republicans failed to achieve a single, tangible policy goal during President Trump's first year in office. The party's dismal performance in power should make everyone wonder whether Republican elites, deep down inside, actually think that their policy prescriptions would lead to Armageddon.

Matthew Flinders, in an eloquent book called *Defending Politics*, argued that voters tend to take for granted the things that democracy has successfully delivered in modern societies. They don't want to hear bad news—things like "We actually need to raise taxes to create universal healthcare." Because politicians are nearly always punished with removal for this kind of honesty, citizens inadvertently create a context where their leaders have an incentive to lie to them and to make extravagant promises. And as Flinders puts it, "No politics has the magic to satisfy a world of greater and greater expectations."[72] Antisystem parties make this problem, which is endemic to even the most successful democracies, far worse. And that is what the GOP has done this century. Their voters believe that they can be delivered more security and greater economic growth while paying less in taxes, and that all of this can be done without touching a hair on the welfare state's head.

Postwar European democracies largely managed their antisystem challengers by allowing them to participate normally in political affairs and run for seats in parliament, gambling that publics would never completely lose control of their senses by actually giving them enough power to govern. Those democracies survived the challenge to their legitimacy and functionality posed by the far right and the far left during this time period. And Sartori took a dim view of their chances in normal political affairs in the long run. Mostly, he was proven right, and over time the parties of the far left in particular became tamed by their participation in politics, often choosing to behave normally to maximize their power rather than sitting so far outside of the system that they had no influence at all. But he also warned that "the political scientist may well have to discover that the 'long run' was too long for the living actors—and for the political system."[73] In other words, he was deeply fearful of what might happen should a crisis or accident put one of these parties in control of the powerful parliamentary machinery of a Continental European society.

The truly terrifying thing about the contemporary Republican Party is not Donald Trump, a man who has proven to be galactically inept in office, someone so incapable of learning, acting maturely, or growing into office that his administration quickly became consumed just by managing his idiocy. Whatever happens to him, the real menace to the future of progress, peace, and civility in the United States is posed by the institutional Republican Party itself. With their systematic torching of important norms of bipartisanship in the Senate and Congress, as well as with their absurd abuses of power, such as spending millions of taxpayer dollars chasing the "scandal" in Benghazi, the GOP has proven that it no longer exists somewhere along the ordinary two-party ideological spectrum in America. Rather, they have morphed into an antisystem party, whose goal is to destroy voter participation and erect a kind of "hybrid democracy" where facade elections are held but where real executive power is not at stake.

This kind of regime goes by many names in political science—"illiberal democracy," "competitive authoritarianism," and more. What links these similar concepts together is that authoritarian insiders in these places conspire to prevent themselves and their allies from ever losing power to their opposition. It's not that no politics take place there, or that executives are unconstrained, but rather that elites use their power to close off the many avenues to change even when their citizens desperately desire it. This is Vladimir Putin's Russia or Viktor Yanukovych's Ukraine or Recep Tayyip Erdoğan's Turkey. If you think it could never happen here in America, you haven't been paying close enough attention to what is happening in Washington, D.C. and in the far-flung provinces of the nation, where local Republican Parties in places like North Carolina have already deployed some of these methods. In the Tarheel State, sitting governor Pat McCrory lost a squeaker of an election to his Democratic challenger Roy Cooper in 2016, only to see the Republican-controlled legislature shamelessly strip the governor's mansion of some of its powers in a series of late-night maneuvers before Cooper took office.[74] The whole sordid fiasco was reminiscent of the Republican-controlled Congress shrinking the Supreme Court to prevent Andrew Johnson from filling vacant seats in 1866.

Tangling with an antisystem party is not easy. While most of the solutions recommended in this book would be applicable and defensible at any time, the following counsel is not. But for the time being, Democrats must avoid their natural instinct to govern and make incremental progress on a host of issues. They must avoid the temptation to work with President Trump or his replacement in office, because doing so would give an enormous advantage to their ideologically minded antisystem opponents. Matt Grossman and David Hopkins, in their book *Asymmetric Politics*, argue that the best way to think about our party system is to understand that the Democratic Party is a coalition of interest groups pursuing discrete policy goals in specific issue areas, whereas the Republican Party is chiefly an ideological vehicle for movement conservatism. Our politics remain fractured owing to a central paradox of how Americans think about ideology and the role of government: They "hold left-of-center views on most specific policy issues while simultaneously preferring conservative positions on broad ideological principles."[75] In other words, Americans respond favorably to ideas like personal responsibility and limited government, even as they, for example, oppose cuts to specific government programs and may even express support for greater government intervention in areas like health care. That basic lack of clarity about what voters want means that they are often going to be vulnerable to appeals from the GOP, who will sell them individual things that they don't actually want, but who speak a language that connects better with their abstract beliefs about politics and society.

Winning that fight is going to take years of messaging and a renewed commitment to defending the role of the state as the only thing standing between voters and the vicissitudes of unrestrained capitalism. But for now, they must win a narrower battle about whether the GOP should continue to be granted the right to rule, convince voters that Republicans are inept and incapable of properly administering the country, and persuade them that Democrats can do a better job. More than anything, they must learn the lessons of the recent past and unlearn the prevailing interpretation of the 1990s—that Bill Clinton was re-elected because the public soured on the antics of Newt Gingrich's GOP and sided with the adults in the room. A mythology has developed around the 1995 government shutdown—that it destroyed the Republicans and put Clinton back into office. This is nonsense. If it was true, the GOP would have been swept out of Congress in 1996 by an enraged public. Clinton won reelection because the economy was humming along like Trump's "fine-tuned machine," and because voters rather liked the compromises that Clinton and Gingrich's GOP had agreed to after Republicans swept Democratic majorities out of Congress in 1994. While they became enormous liabilities for Hillary Clinton in the 2016 primary, welfare reform[76] and the 1994 crime bill were applauded by the public at the time.[77]

The Republicans had made the terrible mistake of making it look like Washington was working, when what they really needed to take down Clinton was to create an ugly, unbearable spectacle of misery and scandal that voters would eventually tire of. What voters saw in 1996 was an arrangement that worked for them: a president who was probably to the left of the country's center of political gravity being guided to the median voter by a congressional GOP that was to its right. They liked it, because it benefitted them, and despite the partisan rancor, things were getting done. To get rid of Clinton, the GOP would have to get much more ruthless with their opponents. This is what happened between 1998 and 2000, when the combined weight of Clinton's impeachment, his sex scandals, and political gravity narrowly delivered the presidency and Congress (temporarily) to the GOP in 2000. Learning the wrong lessons from the 1990s is precisely what undid the Democratic Party after 2000 and especially after 9/11, when compliant and fearful Democrats largely did the bidding of George W. Bush. Democrats gleefully signed up for Bush's crusades. They worked to soften his tax cuts. They gave him political cover for his most disastrous misadventures, all because they were terrified of being painted as soft on national security. Elected Democrats became so despised by their own base that Howard Dean's rebel yell of a campaign slogan in the 2004 primaries—"I'm from the democratic wing of the Democratic party"—reinvigorated the party and catalyzed a move to the left and a renewed obstructionism that helped deliver Congress in 2006 and then the whole ball of wax in 2008.

Ruthless obstruction should be the strategy on the Democratic side of the aisle unless and until the party recaptures one of the branches of Congress. They must resist the temptation to cut deals with the GOP and to normalize and legitimize Trump and his Vichy Republican enablers. Because they are the minority party in both the House and Senate, they need not even make any particularly tough decisions about whether participation in the legislative process might deliver tangible goods to their constituents. Republicans in the House and Senate wrote their cruel Obamacare "replacement" not just behind closed doors[78] but seemingly in a secure bunker capable of surviving a thermonuclear exchange. They held no hearings and tried to jam it through Congress in the dead of night before anyone, including the Congressional Budget Office, could figure out what was actually in the bill. It was a literal caricature of the eighteen-month-long process Democrats pursued to pass the ACA in the first place. And it's not just healthcare. GOP elites have shown zero interest in engaging in any compromise with Democrats outside of the budgeting process, where some minimal collaboration is necessary to prevent the fiscal cliff apocalypse from happening. They don't want Democratic input on tax reform. They don't want it on immigration or border security or consumer protection.

And therefore they must not have it at all.

Senate Democrats may maintain some leverage on a handful of issues because of the lingering presence of the doomed filibuster in the chamber's rules. But mark my words: if Democrats scuttle, say, entitlement reform (which they should) by filibustering it, it will only be a matter of time before the legislative filibuster joins the judicial filibuster in the garbage disposal of history. All Mitch McConnell needs to do is press the button and grind it into liquid capable of traversing the pipes into the sewer. The most important thing for Democrats is not to collaborate. Obstruct, delay, deny. Nothing that Trump wants to do is worth the price of being seen as Trump's handmaidens. Not a garbage infrastructure bill that doubles as an investment bonanza for Wall Street tomb raiders. Not a deal to make Trump's travel policies marginally less horrific. The only exceptions that Democrats should be willing to entertain is participating in negotiations to save vulnerable Americans from Trumpcare, or the Dreamers from deportation. There is some thinking on the left these days that Democrats should just stand aside and let Republicans pass an insanely unpopular healthcare reform bill—the version of Trumpcare on the table in July 2017 was polling, in some cases, 3-to-1 against,[79] and was as close to a political suicide note as any of us alive have ever seen. What senior party leaders could possibly be thinking is almost beyond imagination. But 2018 and 2020 victories must not be won by exploiting the suffering and misery of key Democratic constituencies.

The default negotiating position of the Democratic Party until they regain power in the House or Senate should be this: You will give us Merrick Garland, or you may go die in a fire. Because no such concession will be forthcoming, Democrats must use every bullet in their dwindling chamber to slow down the Trump agenda and grind Congress to an embarrassing, loathsome halt. Tack a billion amendments onto every bill. Withhold consent from even normal, routine Senate procedures, and make preposterous demands in exchange for relenting. Oh, you want a budget? That's cool, but we'll need single-payer healthcare in return. You'd like some Democratic votes for the Border Adjustment Tax? Dope, but in exchange we want an amnesty for every single undocumented immigrant in the United States. You want to slash the corporate tax, right? Aces, but we'll need a Robin Hood tax on financial transactions to make that happen. Use the party's limited negotiating power to show voters that they have real, workable ideas.

The point, then, is not to legislate from the minority. It is to offer the American people a clear, nationalized alternative to the GOP's cruel policy plans for the American people. The only way to take back the House in spite of the devious gerrymander implemented by the Republicans after the 2010 census (see chapter five for more on this) is to turn every single seat in the House and every single seat in the Senate into a referendum on the political state of the country. Demonizing Trump is simply not enough. They must peel away some voters from Trump, even those who applaud the president's morbid Twitter brinksmanship and stick-it-to-the-elites stunts. One reason is a basic paradox identified long ago by political scientists: Americans have generally disapproved of Congress over the past several generations, or at least that's what they tell pollsters. But they also generally like their own congress critter and will vote to reelect him or her. This is known as "Fenno's Paradox."[80] And while this paradox is generally understood to mean that there is no relationship between Congress's popularity as a whole and the fate of individual representatives, this is not true. The two approval ratings do in fact move in tandem. So while voters tend to approve of their own representative at levels higher than their expressed support for Congress as an institution, it's not like there is nothing that can shake their trust in their representative. The more they can throw sand in the gears of the legislative process, the more Democrats will deprive today's congressional Republicans of the only thing they currently have open to them, which is the ability to deliver discrete goods to local constituents in the form of spending.

David Mayhew argued over forty years ago that Congress is "an assembly of professional politicians spinning out political careers. The jobs offer good pay and high prestige. There is no want of applicants for them. Successful pursuit of a career requires continual reelection."[81] Mayhew argued that the desire to be returned to office is the overriding concern of most members of the U.S. Congress. In the past, there were enough "marginal" districts—that is, districts where the outcome depended on small shifts in the national partisan atmosphere—that individual members of Congress had some incentive to work together to solve problems. Today, with only about thirty-six or so genuinely competitive districts in the entire House of Representatives, most individuals are strongly incentivized to make policy that will please their most extreme voters, which are the ones who turn out for partisan primaries. There is little that Democrats can do about that unless they win sweeping power in 2020 (see chapter five), but there is something they can do to make Republican House members less popular in their own districts. And they must: incumbency re-election rates (the percentage of incumbent legislators who are returned to office if they run) were extraordinarily high from the 1960s to the present day. And the reason is that the bipartisanship and ticket-splitting that characterized U.S. politics from the 1950s to the 1980s is long gone and has been replaced by an increase in straight ticket voting. It has become much harder to hold a district in hostile partisan territory than it was twenty or thirty years ago.[82] And because in 2018, the GOP is defending more seats that Clinton won than vice versa (districts that Trump won but are held by a Democrat), Democrats have a distinct advantage in picking up seats even apart from the president's galactic unpopularity.

What they must do, then, is convince their partisans in Clinton districts to toss out the Republican and then hold the Trump seats by capitalizing on the president's toxicity. The figure to keep an eye on is called the "generic congressional ballot" and asks voters whether they would send a Democrat or a Republican to the House if the election were held that day. Because of how deviously the GOP gerrymandered the House after 2010, it would take a Democratic national advantage of anywhere from 7 to 12 points to actually recapture the chamber. Princeton's Sam Wang, who infamously had to eat a bug on live television because he had promised to do so if Trump won, argued that the magic number is 7 percent.[83] Kyle Kondik of Sabato's Crystal Ball (a forecasting and analysis organization) argued the number needs to be closer to 10 percent.[84] Whatever the true magic number for flipping the House is, it is quite clear that Republicans must be extraordinarily unpopular for this to happen as long as the 2010 gerrymander remains in place. As of early January 2018, the *Five Thirty Eight* average of generic ballot polls was Democrats +12.9 percent. These numbers are looking so bad for Republicans that Democrats might even take back the Senate this year despite having to defend ten seats in states won by Donald Trump, some of them by blowout margins. And while the president's party nearly always loses seats in the midterm elections, it is not a sure-fire outcome—Bush's Republicans bucked the trend in 2002, as did Clinton's Democrats in 1998. In both cases, Congress had worked with the president in the recent past to craft major pieces of popular national legislation. Democrats must ensure that Trump is isolated, alone, embattled, and has not a single legislative victory with a single Democratic fingerprint on it. And they must keep their activists engaged in the fight—swarming town halls, dialing their representatives, running for office themselves, and committed to total obstruction.

Since the election, the organization leading the obstruction charge is called Indivisible. A group of battle-hardened Hill staffers formed the group in the dispiriting wake of Black Tuesday and quickly released a guide to fighting back, called *The Indivisible Guide*, which takes as its starting point the activism of the Tea Party that helped derail the Obama presidency. "We saw them organize locally and convince their own MoCs to reject President Obama's agenda. Their ideas were wrong, cruel, and tinged with racism—and they won," write the authors.[85] Since Trump took office, these tactics, including flooding the offices of wavering Republicans with phone calls, showing up to Town Halls and contesting key pieces of legislation publicly and visiting local offices in person, either to make your displeasure known or to reinforce the Democratic troops fighting the good fight, have created new and tangible energy on the left. They've done so by adopting some of the organizational innovation on display in the Tea Party right during the Obama years. "Organizing," Ezra Levin, one of Indivisible's cofounders, told me, "is about building local leadership and power through local leadership. It's why for Indivisible we feel really strongly that the unit of activism is—not—the individual."[86] Since the organization launched in January 2017, it has cultivated over 6,000 local chapters, where they hope that organizing leadership will survive the high-energy moments, like the one surrounding Trumpcare, to be an ongoing force for change.

But in addition to their work mobilizing and organizing citizens, Indivisible is also advising Democrats on how they can use parliamentary procedure to jam up the Republican agenda, in ways that require support from the grassroots but that fundamentally depend on decisions made in Washington by the party's leadership. One important example of these tactics was revealed in a tweetstorm by Levin on June 15, 2016. He identified a hole in the GOP strategy to pass an Obamacare repeal through the "reconciliation" process, which allows legislation to go through the Senate on a simple majority rather than with sixty-plus votes. Levin argued that the rules of reconciliation votes also require something called a "vote-a-rama" in which senators may propose limitless amendments to the legislation. Each of these amendments must be considered and voted up. "If @SenateDems introduce 1,000 amendments, that's 10,000 minutes. 10,000 minutes = 167 hours = 7 days. So 1,000 amendments = 1 week," Levin wrote in a post that was retweeted almost 9,000 times.

Democrats actually got religion on Senate obstructionism during the health care fight. Minority leader Chuck Schumer, under pressure from Indivisible and other activists, announced that until Senate Republicans returned to regular order in the Senate for the health care debate that Democrats would do everything they could to slow all proceedings in the Senate. For one thing, Democrats are withholding consent even for routine executive branch nominations. By requiring a cloture vote on every single vote, Democrats can drag out nominations even though sixty votes are no longer required for presidential appointments, federal judicial nominations, or Supreme Court picks. As Carl Hulse wrote in July 2017, after cloture is invoked, "An 'intervening day' is then required to allow the cloture request to 'ripen.' Next is a vote to impose cloture followed by thirty hours of 'post-cloture' debate before a final vote."[87] By placing holds on every single thing that Mitch McConnell intends to bring up for a vote, Democrats can force their adversaries to burn so much precious floor time that they can put the GOP's legislative agenda into bumper-to-bumper traffic. When I asked Ezra Levin why McConnell hadn't simply changed the rules to shorten debate post-cloture, he told me, "There are also a number of old-timer Republicans who are defenders of the filibusters and Senate procedures. For something like changing rules around cloture, I could see him just not having the votes."[88] For the time being then, Democrats can continue to use these slowing procedures, not just to make a point about process—that Republicans wrote the health care bill in secret and limited debate to almost nothing—but as a permanent fixture of their opposition strategy throughout the Trump Administration, or until they are returned to a majority in the House, Senate, or both.

While there are a few such tricks left in the Democratic quiver, as the minority in both chambers and absent party-switching, Democrats may have to get used to losing policy battles until the 2018 midterms. Nevertheless, they should leave it all out on the field, as they did with the Gorsuch nomination, when they successfully filibustered Baby Scalia and forced McConnell to eliminate the judicial filibuster for Supreme Court nominations. Ideally, Democrats at some point will force the GOP to nuke the legislative filibuster once and for all. And that points to something that is important to keep in mind—once the GOP trashes these longstanding bipartisan norms—about the necessity of placing bills in committee, about holding a certain amount of debate for bills, about seeking input from the opposition, they are extinguished forever.

And when the Democrats ride triumphant into D.C. they will not be obligated to resurrect them. This is not to say that they should make major changes to policy without debate, but nor should they be bound by the rules and norms that existed at the turn of this century. They will make laws with simple majorities, they will fast-track legislation, and they will close the doors and send the Republicans home to toy with their fantasy football teams. They should change the Senate rules to deprive the GOP of any right to input of any kind on anything that is happening in the chamber. One of their very first moves should be to drastically cut the time allotted to debate after cloture is invoked, so that Republicans do not infinitely delay major nominations or bills. They should reduce the number of hours of required debate in the House.

Democrats should not, as Republicans did with Trumpcare, totally avoid the committee process, whereby all bills are first directed to the appropriate committee for hearings and markup—not just because this is a bad enough process that the toxicity actually reaches voters who normally wouldn't care, but because it would lead to bad policy. But they should substantially reduce any opportunity the minority might have to influence those proceedings by changing the Senate and House rules to deprive the minority of any opportunities to extend debate, make amendments, and slow down routine legislative processes. Again, this is not just good policy for the Democrats, but a necessary reform for governance. And because Democrats will, I hope, have dozens of bills ready to roll when they are next given the opportunity to govern, they could have the most productive, transformative first one hundred days since FDR. And if anyone asks why they are doing it like this, and why they aren't asking for Mitch McConnell's permission or genuflecting before a bipartisanship that has, in the famous words of Monty Python's Parrot Shop sketch, "rung down the curtain and joined the choir invisible," they can fire back with the famous quip from the best '80s-era antidrug commercial ever made, when a father forces his weed-smoking son to admit that "I learned it by watching you, OK? *I learned it by watching you.*"

Yes, there is some danger of obliterating these rules and norms only to lose both chambers of Congress back to the GOP in the next election. Democrats got a taste of this when they eliminated the judicial filibuster for district and appellate court nominees in 2013, and then watched the Republicans escalate after retaking power by stonewalling President Obama's Supreme Court nominee, Merrick Garland, in 2016 and then nuking the filibuster for Supreme Court nominees in 2017. But there are two reasons to press forward: first, Republicans have proven time and again that they will work to dismantle norms, unwritten rules, and easily changeable chamber rules at the first possible opportunity. If Democrats don't do it, their adversaries will. More to the point of this book, progressives are likely to hold power more often than the GOP if they heed the advice below and systematically address the Left's structural deficits in the American electoral system. Risking an increase in bad policy when Republicans run the government is worthwhile if and only if other changes to the U.S. political system are implemented simultaneously, to give Democrats (and hopefully smaller progressive parties) an even electoral playing field.

The best way for individuals to hold Democratic elected officials accountable and to make sure that they give their adversaries no quarter, is to join groups like Indivisible (which now has thousands of local chapters), MoveOn, and Democracy For America, as well as progressive groups like the Democratic Socialists of America. These organizations lead the charge during legislative fights by coordinating action across the country. Show up to protests and town halls and be noisy. As Levin told me, "It's relatively easy to ignore ten people or fifty people. It's much more difficult to ignore five, ten, or fifty people if tens of thousands of people will see that action."[89] Make sure that in addition to calling your GOP representatives and begging them again and again not to kill you, that you also place the occasional call to Democratic or independent offices and thank them for voting the right way and keeping the party together. And above all, donate as much of your time and your money as you possibly can to state and national elections in 2018 and 2020—if Democrats aren't swept into power in the next two cycles, nothing outlined in this book will be possible anyway, and the United States will continue lurching toward insolvency, catastrophe, planetary disaster, and violence.

If Democrats and their progressive allies are able to carry this strategy out, they should be rewarded with the opportunity to govern. And if they are, the very first major legislative thing they should do is ram through a set of bills increasing the number of states in the union from fifty to fifty-eight.

★ 3 ★

# The 58-State Solution

## GIVE THE SWAMP STATEHOOD

On June 14, 2017, in a not-quite-air-conditioned-enough second-floor room of a bar called the Big Board on H Street, a crew of thirty or so activists, lawyers, and community leaders gathered to hear about issues of criminal justice reform in the District of Columbia. Three speakers addressed the crowd about issues ranging from the Neighborhood Engagement Achieves Results Act (NEAR) to the impending construction of a new prison for the district, financed through a public-private partnership. And while most of the evening was spent sorting through political issues faced by activists everywhere—how to secure funding, how to push back against corporate encroachment on public services, how to strong arm the municipal government into cooperating—there was one significant overarching issue that came up again and again: the unique, bizarre, and unjustifiable political status of Washington, D.C. itself. "This is a statehood issue," said one veteran activist named Elinor Hart. A public interest attorney named Emily Tatro noted that the federalization of prisons in D.C. is a huge and unappreciated problem, with inmates being shipped around to federal facilities all around the country, needlessly and cruelly dividing families from one another. As the district is 49 percent African American, it is hard not to see in these practices echoes of slavery's most inhumane procedures.

But for the moment, these activists remain trapped by the grim reality of America's weirdest and most unfair political system.

If you've ever spent any time in the nation's swamp capital, one of the first things you're likely to notice is the District's smart-aleck license plates, which read "Taxation Without Representation." The cheeky plates were one of the Clinton Administration's parting gifts to its residents, a middle finger to the capital's status as a non-state with no voting representation in Congress. They were replaced by the Bush Administration, which was hostile to D.C. statehood for reasons that should be obvious, and reinstituted by the Obama Administration in 2009. They have become a lower-stakes version of the Global Gag Rule on abortion that is implemented by Republican presidents and rescinded by their Democratic counterparts.

Although a license plate does not a political project make, it identifies a very real and very indefensible problem: the 600,000 plus residents of Washington D.C. have no voting representation whatsoever in the United States Congress. D.C. sends just one, non-voting representative to the House. It's not nothing, but it's unforgivable from any perspective in democratic theory. Worse, D.C. as a city—a place inhabited by actual human beings who should have the same rights to representation and competent public administration as the rest of us—is criminally harmed by the inability of the city government to, for example, impose a tax on the hundreds of thousands of rich commuters who pour into the district from Virginia and Maryland, or to raise sufficient funds to keep the city's critical Metro system functioning properly. Decades of vociferous, meticulous, and clever activism around D.C.'s political status have worked to unify the city's citizens in favor of admission to the union as a state, but at the same time has so far failed even to engage the town's natural allies—Democrats and progressives—in a coherent project to change the status quo.

Doing so is a matter of national urgency. Throughout this book, I argue that Democrats and progressives face structural, rather than just policy or demographic challenges in winning and holding power in national American politics. One of the most persistent and problematic is the natural deficit that Democrats currently face in the United States Senate. As E.J. Dionne, Norman Ornstein, and Thomas Mann note, "Because more-populated states tend to vote Democratic, the 48 Democrats actually represent 55 percent of the nation's population."[90] With roughly thirty Republican-leaning states and twenty Democratic-leaning states, the Constitution's unchangeable writ that each state have an equal number of senators means that no matter how many more votes Democrats get nationally, they are going to win the Senate only during wave election years, and then probably only for a relatively brief period of time. Therefore, to make any lasting changes to U.S. politics and society, Democrats are going to have to admit more states to the union and create further entities out of the ones that already exist. And they must start with Washington, D.C.

Washington, D.C. is an eighteenth-century creation, whose status as an entity ruled entirely (at first) by Congress was justified by the Framers' fears that having the nation's capital in the territory of an existing state would give that state undue advantage over the others. "The issue," writes Tom Lewis, "traded on the fear that the seat of democratic government might soon resemble one of the corrupt large European capitals, such as London."[91] Article I, Section 8 of the U.S. Constitution very clearly grants Congress the right to exercise exclusive jurisdiction over the capital city. As with so many compromises made to placate state governments, little thought was given at the time to the rights of the District's (then nonexistent) citizens, who until the Twenty-third Amendment was ratified by the states in 1961, were not even allowed to vote for the president. The idea—quaint even at the time, and preposterous today—was that just being in the proximity of the federal government would be enough for D.C. residents to have their voices and concerns heard. As if you're walking down Pennsylvania Avenue and James Monroe comes perambulating toward you with a copy of the *Federalist Papers* tucked under his arm and you hail him with: "Jimmy, don't let the Europeans muck about with Latin America!" And Madison responds, "Tally ho, fellow citizen! It is so wonderful that we're here in the city together and I think you make a very good point!" And thus was born the Monroe Doctrine.

In reality, of course, Washington, D.C. developed into one of the most stratified, segregated cities in the country, and statehood for Washington, D.C. is that rarest of creatures in politics: It is both the right thing to do as well as an easy win for Democrats moving forward. Voters there favored Hillary Clinton over Donald Trump by an astonishing 93–4 margin, with the future impeachment case study and human scandal machine barely outpolling the catatonic drug legalization crusader Gary Johnson of the Libertarian Party. The District's nonvoting Democratic House member, Eleanor Holmes Norton, was returned 89–4 and the GOP did not bother running a candidate. And the statehood referendum on the ballot that year passed by an overwhelming 86–14 margin. This is clearly what the people of D.C. want, it rectifies the unconscionable lack of voting rights for the city's citizens, it will give the Democrats two Senate seats that a *Politico* intern could win in a cakewalk, and it will also give the party an extra seat in the House (or more, if Democrats follow my advice below). So why has it never happened, particularly during one of the periods where Democrats control Congress and the presidency?

The last successful push to expand voting rights for D.C. came decades ago, when Congress passed and the states ratified in 1961 the Twenty-third Amendment to the Constitution, which grants the District electors in the Electoral College equivalent to the number it would have if it were a state. In 1973, Congress passed the District of Columbia Home Rule Act, which gave the city a small council and an elected mayor. While these two changes certainly improved the voting rights of the city's residents, they still had no representation in Congress. Despite agreeing in 1971 to seat a nonvoting delegate in the House from D.C., that person has no structural power and has no vote for actual legislation in Congress. These piecemeal efforts suggest that D.C.'s democratic deficit is well-known and recognized in the corridors of power, but that no one has been willing to take the next step of actually doing something about it.

The most recent and serious effort to grant statehood for the capital took place during the early days of the Clinton Administration, when a statehood bill actually made it out of committee only to die decisively in a 277–153 defeat. Statehood supporters knew at the time that the bill was going down. The District's non–voting House delegate then as now was Eleanor Holmes Norton, a former assistant director of the American Civil Liberties Union and Jimmy Carter's director of the Equal Opportunity Employment Commission. Norton argued at the time that even a massive defeat on the House floor "would give the undemocratic treatment of the District the serious national attention it would never attract in any other way."[92] About this she was probably wrong. It would be twenty years before another bill even got a hearing. Dana Rohrabacher (R-CA), told *The Washington Post* that if D.C. is granted statehood, then he should be allowed to "make Orange County into four states."[93] (More on that later, Dana.) Even in a somewhat less-polarized time, Republicans realized that statehood for the District would give the Democrats, no doubt about it, Senate and House seats. GOP operatives depicted the initiative as a Democratic power grab. Floyd Brown, the man partially responsible for the infamous Willie Horton attack ad during the 1988 presidential campaign, put out a mailer claiming that the statehood would "guarantee a U.S. Senate seat for Jesse Jackson."[94]

*Quelle horreur!* But this racist appeal was no outlier. The campaign against statehood was openly bigoted, with the terrifying specter of a (gasp!) majority-minority state hanging over the white-dominated Congress. During the House debate, Rep. Tom DeLay

(R-TX) criticized the District's "hug-a-thug attitude on violent crime" as one reason to oppose statehood, an obviously racialized appeal.[95] Unsurprisingly, the remaining contingent of Southern Democrats in the House was largely responsible for spiking a bill that would have enhanced their own party's prospects—all five Democrats from Alabama and Arkansas (all white) voted no. Three out of four Mississippi Democrats (all white) voted no.[96] With a handful of exceptions, the only Democratic support from the South came from African-American Democrats. That was fitting, because the existence of Democrats in the American South was about to end in a series of wave elections starting the following year in 1994 and then culminating in the GOP's obliteration of the brief Democratic House majority in 2010.

Another argument against D.C. statehood made by the kind of people who seem to have a bias-confirming quote from the *Federalist Papers* handy for every occasion, was that it was "too urban" to be a real state, as if somewhere there is a manual for what states should look like and that it calls for a perfect balance between pavement and farmland. There are whole countries that are cities (Hello, Singapore!). If there are entire states, like North Dakota, that are basically bereft of an actual city, there is no reason that one of our states can't be a medium-sized metropolis. There is nothing in the Constitution to prevent it nor even any particularly good arguments against such an arrangement. Nor is D.C. too small in terms of population to be a state. This objection was raised, preposterously, by Rohrabacher in the House proceedings when he argued that "My State has fifty times the population of this area, and it is not fair to them to give the District of Columbia two U.S. Senators."[97] While true, this disparity already exists, and D.C. would not even be the smallest state in the union. Wyoming and Vermont have smaller populations than the District, and Alaska, North Dakota, South Dakota, and Delaware all have fewer than a million residents. No one is angling to take their two senators away.

The failure of D.C. statehood in 1993 should perhaps not surprise us too much, even if the actual record of the debates is painful to look at. But why did Democrats not make a push for it when they possessed a filibuster-proof majority in the Senate prior to the death of Ted Kennedy, and significant margins in the House? Part of the answer is that the statehood process requires a series of steps, and the reality is that statehood proponents did not have their ducks in a row in 2009. For Congress to pass a statehood bill, the district's citizens must first express their support for the measure in a referendum. And Obama and congressional Democrats were, at the time, understandably preoccupied with the incredibly complex negotiations surrounding the Affordable Care Act and the overhaul of the country's financial system that ended with the passage of Dodd-Frank. The window of opportunity turned out to be painfully short—once the House was lost in the 2010 midterms, statehood became a dead letter for the foreseeable future, as no Republican is likely to vote for any measure that increases the structural power of their ideological opponents, even if it is unquestionably the moral path to pursue. And because of the GOP's diabolical plan to gerrymander the House out of competitiveness (discussed more fully in chapter five), statehood debates became theoretical and would remain so until it seemed possible to imagine a fully unified Democratic government in D.C.—a possibility that was tangible and tantalizing for parts of 2016, particularly when Hillary Clinton's polling lead and Donald Trump's unpopularity threatened to put the House and Senate in play for Democrats.

Statehood is a particularly sacred goal for Michael Brown, one of D.C.'s two "shadow senators" dutifully elected by voters. Brown, who has an ID that says "United States Senator," nevertheless has no actual power. Over lunch at the National Democratic Club on a tree-lined D.C. side street, Brown told me that his existence depends "on the kindness of strangers."[98] In a room filled with other Democratic dignitaries, all of whom have the actual power to introduce legislation and vote on it, Brown is a curiosity. A gregarious sixty-something, Brown got his start campaigning for Jimmy Carter and operated a profitable D.C. lobbying shop before running for his fake seat in 2006. Few Americans understand the concept of "shadow" anything, nor do many people understand D.C.'s predicament. Brown has no staff, no office, and a tiny budget provided by the city. He is mostly there for show, but he says he works hard to represent the interests of his constituents, and that he's not just an elaborate stunt put on by the District's leaders. But the District's dependence on Congress for budgeting leads to deeply destructive outcomes for residents. Congress can, says Brown, intervene in local budgeting affairs to strip individual items out of the District's budget. And the city, which is dependent on its Metro rail system for functioning, can't tax commuters as many cities do for the privilege of living or working in the city. "It's estimated that we lose $3 billion a year," he says, due to the city's inability to tax income at its source. Brown tells a story of how every year for ten years Congress spiked a needle exchange program designed to address the AIDS epidemic. "Congress can put riders on the budget," he says—a parliamentary maneuver where you attach a "poison pill" provision to kill legislation. "They have absolute control."

Brown's largely ceremonial office is part of a D.C. effort to imitate the so-called "Tennessee Plan," by which the then-territory of Tennessee held a constitutional convention, elected representatives to office (long before they had the right to be seated), and basically dared Congress not to recognize them.[99] During his time in "office," Brown has seen the statehood movement grow from a fringe organization with no real plan to a group that has ratified a state constitution and a statehood referendum, according to well-established procedures by which other states have joined the union. When that happens, D.C.'s city government would become its state government, with the mayor herself transformed, Cindarella-style, into a governor and the city council magically alchemized into a unicameral state legislature. "It takes a single majority vote and a signature from the president, and we're done," Brown argues.

But the language of Article I, Section 8 does create some headaches for statehood proponents, not least in that it unambiguously grants Congress permanent control over the "seat of government of the United States." It reads, "To exercise exclusive legislation in all cases whatsoever, over such District (not exceeding ten miles square) as may, by cession of particular states, and the acceptance of Congress, become the seat of the government of the United States, and to exercise like authority over all places purchased by the consent of the legislature of the state in which the same shall be, for the erection of forts, magazines, arsenals, dockyards, and other needful buildings." Brown is dismissive of this argument, typically made by statehood opponents. "My response is that I don't give a damn," he quips before launching into an explanation of why the Framers created a federal district in the first place. In 1783, Revolutionary War veterans rioted in Philadelphia near the existing capital, and the government of Pennsylvania refused to help. "Madison said we have to be in control of whatever jurisdiction we reside in so that doesn't happen again," Brown explained.

The D.C. statehood bill finds an easy workaround to this problem, by maintaining federal control over a small portion of the District—the Capitol, the Supreme Court, the Senate and House buildings, and more—while turning over the rest of the territory, where humans actually live, to the new state government of what proponents have long called New Columbia. It means, functionally, shrinking the capitol district called for by the Constitution to the bare minimum and leaving the rest for the new D.C. state. The argument advanced by statehood opponents that the federal district cannot be less than ten square miles in size is plainly absurd. Just go reread the actual language of the Constitution. I'll wait. It says it can't *exceed* ten square miles, not that it must *be* ten square miles. Other constitutional fetishists also claim that D.C. would need to get permission from Maryland. The Cato Institute's Roger Pilon argues, "Just as the original creation of the District required the consent of the contributing states, so too, as with all agreements, does any change in the terms of that grant require the consent of the parties—and Maryland has given no indication that it would consent to having a new state created on its border from what was formerly part of the state. At the least, previous proposals have received little support from the free state."[100]

Even if this were true, and statehood proponents generally dismiss this argument as a trifle, it is not clear why heavily Democratic Maryland would object to a plot that would clearly increase the institutional power of the Democratic Party. If anything, the state might welcome the opportunity to work with another state that has real control of its budget on issues like the Metro, which is shared between D.C., Maryland, and Virginia. Such multistate commissions are not unusual, such as the Delaware River Port Authority, which manages crossings between New Jersey and Pennsylvania. And Marylanders would certainly prefer D.C. statehood to any plot that seeks to return the residential areas of the district to the control of Annapolis. (This plan, so beloved by Republicans because it would avoid the creation of two new Democratic Senators, reminds me a lot of the "Jordan is Palestine" plan to resolve the Israeli-Palestinian conflict by attaching the West Bank to Jordan, a country that is already heavily Palestinian.)

In short, while there will be lawsuits (there are always lawsuits), there is very little standing in the way of statehood for D.C. besides Republican control of the government. If Democrats do not vigorously pursue it when they retake that power, they will have only themselves to blame for kicking away an opportunity to easily increase their structural power in American politics.

## AN UNINCORPORATED TERRITORY IN A NATION

If the predicament of Beltway voters strikes you as bad, it's nothing compared to the plight of Puerto Ricans, who have remained on the sidelines of progress in the United States ever since America took control of the island. The subservient and ambiguous status of Puerto Rico was brought into sharp relief by the devastation wrought in September 2017 by Hurricanes Irma and Maria. Although President Trump and the Federal Emergency Management Agency responded capably to the havoc and human misery inflicted in Texas, Louisiana, and Florida by Hurricanes Harvey and Irma, the government's response to Puerto Rico was appalling—half-hearted, slow, and punitive. The devastated island was largely without power or potable water for months after Maria made landfall as a Category 5.

The president, predictably, made matters worse by arguing that Puerto Ricans "want everything done for them when it should be a community effort," an astonishingly cruel and racist attack that would never be leveled at anyone on the mainland. He later publicly attacked and humiliated the mayor of San Juan, complained that the crisis was busting America's budget, warned islanders that they'd have to pay back Wall Street creditors before seeing any real aid, and congratulated himself and his administration for a job well done despite widespread evidence that the federal response was completely inadequate. Throughout the crisis, the president betrayed a gaping lack of empathy for Puerto Ricans, and inadvertently revealed to the rest of the country the problematic nature of the relationship between the island and the mainland. One poll confirmed the obvious: only 47 percent of respondents know that Puerto Ricans are American citizens,[101] which would explain the broad lack of concern about the island's welfare and future.

Why is this?

The United States assumed control of Puerto Rico after the Spanish-American War of 1898. Since then the question of the relationship between the United States and Puerto Rico has bedeviled even well-intentioned people. Puerto Ricans are certainly less firmly committed to joining the union than Beltway voters. As Amílcar Antonio Barreto argues, "The status question, the incessant debate over remaining a US Commonwealth, seeking independence, or becoming the fifty-first state, dominates its partisan life."[102] However, recent developments have the island careening toward joining the union as a state. On Sunday, June 11, 2017, Puerto Rico held a referendum on whether to seek admission to the union as a state. Statehood proponents won with an astonishing 97 percent of the vote, though with only 23 percent turnout and several opposition parties boycotting the proceedings, including the party that supports independence for the island as a separate country, the message sent by voters was not as clear as it might have been with higher turnout. However, it was the second time in five years that voters approved of statehood as the solution preferred by the most voters on the island. There is not a scintilla of evidence suggesting that a majority or even a plurality of citizens prefer a different option, such as continuing with the current status or seeking independence.

The story of how Puerto Rico got into this mess in the first place is relatively little known. Once a holding of the vast Spanish Empire, the island was, um . . . "ceded" . . . to the United States following the brief 1898 Spanish-American War, a conflict that was started on a flimsy, Gulf-of-Tonkin-like pretext that turned out to be dubious at best—the sinking of the U.S.S. *Maine* in Havana harbor on February 15, 1898. The warship had been sent to Cuba as part of U.S. President McKinley's efforts to find a peaceful resolution to the Cuban revolt against the Spanish crown, at a time when there was considerable public fervor in the United States against Spanish tyranny and in favor of independence for Cuba. Later investigations suggested that the explosion of the *Maine* was probably internal and not an act of war by Spanish forces. But at the time, it didn't matter—the opportunity to lay claim to Spanish holdings in the Caribbean and the Pacific was simply too delicious to pass up. In the ensuing war, which destroyed the vestiges of Spanish imperialism and instantly transformed the United States into a globe-spanning colonial power, Spain ceded Cuba, Puerto Rico, Guam, and the Philippines to the United States.

Despite being recently granted greater autonomy by the Spanish, Puerto Ricans initially greeted the U.S. takeover with hope that the island would either be granted independence or incorporated directly into the United States.[103] Instead, the United States chose a kind of worst-of-both-worlds path for Puerto Rico, granting the island neither a path to statehood as had been followed by so many territories in the past, nor a chance to become an independent sovereign nation. The legal limbo into which American leaders plunged Puerto Rico more than a century ago still persists, curiously and destructively, today. The Foraker Act of 1900 declared Puerto Rico "an overseas possession subject to the plenary power of the US Congress, but did not commit Congress to extend either independence or statehood to the island."[104] The rationale was the same as it was for the Europeans who imposed the Mandate system on the Middle East—the natives were not fit to rule themselves and must pass through a period of colonial tutelage. Or as Republican Senator Joseph B. Foraker put it, "They have no experience which would qualify them for the great work of government."[105]

It may not surprise you to learn that successive U.S. leaders and their viceroys in Puerto Rico treated the actual humans who lived there rather poorly. They sent a never-ending stream of white dudes to rule the island like it was William Taft's vacation home. They transformed Puerto Rico's economy by destroying the coffee industry and making its economy dependent on exporting raw materials to the United States. Under the Foraker Act, the president of the United States appointed virtually the entire administrative structure of Puerto Rico. It meant that when the Americans came, Puerto Ricans enjoyed less freedom than they had only recently been granted by the Spanish in 1897. It was a combustible situation. To make matters worse, the U.S. Supreme Court devised an entire new legal doctrine to deal with the territories acquired from the Spanish, in the so-called "Insular Cases." The Court ruled that the U.S. Constitution does not apply to Puerto Rico and other "unincorporated territories." The Jones Act of 1917 improved on this situation by granting U.S. citizenship to all Puerto Ricans and giving the island an elected legislature, but still denied Puerto Ricans executive control of their territory and deprived them of voting representation in Congress. (It also, as was discovered after Hurricane Maria, hampered relief efforts by preventing foreign aid ships from dispensing aid to the island.) Congress could overrule any act passed by the elected Puerto Rican legislature.[106] It was no coincidence that this legislation passed a month before the U.S entry into World War I: critics charged it was just a vehicle to get Puerto Ricans into the military to fight Germans.[107] Not content merely to impose U.S. rule on Puerto Rico, the United States also engaged in acts of cultural warfare, including making it a felony to own or display the Puerto Rican flag.[108]

For a relatively brief period starting in the 1930s, the Puerto Rican nationalist movement—dedicated to independence for the island rather than a deeper association with the United States—had the energy and the momentum. But U.S. authorities railroaded the nationalist leader Pedro Albizu Campos for the assassination of Puerto Rico's police chief, Col. Francis E. Riggs, in 1937 and sent him to prison for ten years. When he was released in 1947, he found the island's governor more interested in economic development than independence. J. Edgar Hoover sent an enormous FBI detail to follow Albizu around and treated the Puerto Rican nationalists like insurrectionists. The island's bought-and-paid-for governor helped pass Gag Law 53, which once again made displaying the Puerto Rican flag a crime and was designed to make it easier to arrest any nationalist anywhere for any reason. On October 30, 1950, nationalist leaders hurriedly launched an insurrection, believing that the FBI and insular authorities were preparing to move against them. That revolt was ruthlessly suppressed, and the nationalist movement has never really recovered. While a Marxist nationalist group called the Fuerzas Armadas de Liberación Nacional Puertorriqueña (the Armed Forces of National Liberation) conducted a bombing campaign in the United States during the 1970s and early 1980s, there is no evidence that the FALN ever commanded substantial support inside Puerto Rico. As with other so-called "urban guerrilla" campaigns during that time period, like the Red Army Faction in Germany and the Red Brigades in Italy, tactics of indiscriminate violence alienated the very people who were supposed to join the fight. Indeed, the violence discredited Puerto Rican nationalism as an organized force in both American and Puerto Rican public life.

In 1952, President Harry Truman pushed for a referendum on granting Puerto Rico commonwealth status—a more robust form of self-rule that nevertheless did not resolve the underlying dilemma about the territory's ultimate disposition. The new status gave Puerto Rico a fully elected territorial government, including a legislature and governor and gave the island the right to set its own budget, while most other aspects of sovereignty were reserved for the U.S. federal government. On a basic level, Puerto Rico's status has remained unchanged in any meaningful sense since 1952. The bargain between island elites and the United States was underpinned by "Operation Bootstrap," which used tax incentives to lure manufacturing to Puerto Rico, and led to an economic boom in the 1950s and 1960s. For a long period after WWII, those committed to the "commonwealth status" of the island had an upper hand over both statehood and independence proponents. That began to change in the '70s, when high oil prices eroded the incentives for companies to relocate to the island, and when Puerto Rico's phenomenal growth slowed down. Outgoing President Gerald Ford released a statement on December 31, 1976, which included an unambiguous declaration of support for statehood:

> The common bonds of friendship, tradition, dignity, and individual freedom have joined the people of the United States and the people of Puerto Rico. It is now time to make these bonds permanent through statehood in accordance with the concept of mutual acceptance which has historically governed the relationship between Puerto Rico and the United States.[109]

Ford might have been a lame duck, but President Jimmy Carter was also sympathetic to statehood. Indeed, all presidents since Ford have promised to respect the wishes of the island's citizens. The trouble is that Congress maintains the right to make that final status determination and has shown no real intention of doing so—Democrats are just as guilty of neglect here as Republicans.[110] Even Donald Trump has paid some lip service to the idea of Puerto Rico statehood. "The will of the Puerto Rican people in any status referendum should be considered as Congress follows through on any desired change in status for Puerto Rico, including statehood," he said during the campaign in a statement that was far too coherent to be drafted by the future president personally. Yet political leadership keeps kicking the can back to the island, offering them confusing guidance about how to conduct final status referenda, and, puzzlingly, not really acting on any of them or promising to act after a clear result. In some ways the behavior of Congress seems intentionally crafted to produce divisions in Puerto Rico itself and to prevent the emergence of a clear majority for statehood.

Puerto Ricans have birthright citizenship and freedom of movement in the United States. Once they become citizens of any other state, they of course can vote in federal elections. But they are bound by the decisions made by the U.S. president despite having no say in his or her election. The biggest current problem for the island is fiscal. The island was devastated by two twin shocks this century—in 2005, certain tax exemptions for U.S. companies operating out of Puerto Rico expired, having an immediate and devastating impact on the local economy. Between 1996, when Congress began phasing out tax exemptions, and 2014, nearly a decade after they fully expired, manufacturing jobs dropped nearly in half.[111] Unemployment remains higher than in any state, and about 45 percent of the population is below the federal poverty line. The Great Recession hit the island harder than even some other places, and unlike most U.S. states, Puerto Rico has yet to fully recover; its municipalities and agencies cannot file for bankruptcy. But more problematic is the islanders' lack of political voting rights in the United States. Like Washington, D.C., Puerto Rico has only one, nonvoting member of the House of Representatives and, of course, no senators. Unlike D.C., Puerto Rico does not get votes in the Electoral College. If it did, George W. Bush would likely never have been elected president in 2000. Think about that for a second. In 2016, Puerto Ricans experienced a fresh betrayal when Congress appointed a fiscal control board to oversee the island's debt and claimed the right for that board to overturn laws passed by Puerto Rico's legislature.[112]

One of the difficulties for statehood proponents is that the idea has opponents in two directions—in the United States, ascendant white nationalists will object to the very idea of incorporating a Spanish-speaking territory into the United States. The language argument is an old staple of discourse seeking to perpetuate the status quo. Writing in *Orbis*, the late political scientist Alvin Rubinstein[113] argued that "Accepting Puerto Rico as a state would open a Pandora's box of linguistic, political, ethnic, racial, and religious tensions greater than any this nation has ever experienced."[114] Reminiscent of the nineteenth-century rhetoric from both elected officials and the Supreme Court about how the Puerto Ricans were unfit to rule themselves and too different from mainstream America to ever fit in, the language objection is little more than a vehicle disguising the true source of right-wing antipathy to the island, which is race. However, the language objection is a smokescreen—the United States does not have an official language, and thus what to "do" about a majority-Spanish speaking territory is neither here nor there. Puerto Ricans, in their new state, would have the same right as Floridians or New Mexicans to determine precisely how to navigate the complexities of bilingualism. Other societies, including Canada and Belgium, have successfully soldiered on despite containing two distinct national peoples.

And in Puerto Rico, there is a significant minority that would prefer independence to statehood. How large that minority is remains an open question, because the pro-independence parties boycotted the 2017 plebiscite. Simmering anger about the imposition of financial terms by Congress certainly did not help either. Finally, even the pro–status quo party, the Popular Democratic Party (PDP), boycotted the 2017 referendum, precisely because it included a straight status quo option, whereas the PDP supports something called a "Free Associated State." For those reasons and more, it is highly likely that any act by Congress leading to statehood would require yet another referendum on Puerto Rico's status. Such a referendum is a matter of moral necessity even if technically Democrats in Congress could alter Puerto Rico's status without one. While the 97 percent support for statehood is overwhelming, considered in the context of 22 percent turnout, it is of dubious legitimacy. For the sake of simplicity and to obtain majority support for a final determination, that referendum should include just two options: statehood, or independence. Alternately, the referendum could employ a version of ranked-choice voting called the Alternative Vote or Instant Runoff Voting (IRV). Citizens could be asked to rank order their choices—status quo, independence, statehood and some form of free association. In IRV voting, the lowest first-place vote-getter is eliminated and the second preference on those ballots redistributed to the remaining options. This was the system that the United Kingdom rejected in its national 2011 referendum. Such an option would both (a) produce a majority for *something* even in the context of a referendum with multiple choices and (b) give advocates of all four options the opportunity to win.

If anything, Puerto Ricans should be worried about what might happen to their culture after integration into the United States. For decades prior to the annexation of Hawaii by Congress in 1898, white settlers systematically demolished the native government of the island's indigenous people, who had established an independent republic and who had sought in vain to have it recognized by the great powers. From the declaration of Hawaii as an incorporated territory of the United States in 1900, which set it on a path to statehood to its incorporation into the union in 1959, native Hawaiians experienced continued discrimination and dispossession by colonial U.S. elites.[115] Since statehood, some native Hawaiians have increasingly come to regard a kind of nationhood as a potential avenue to relieve the economic and social suffering of their people, who are, like so many other minority populations in the United States, incarcerated at higher rates than whites and experience worse health outcomes, among a variety of other problems. The difference here is that in Puerto Rico, a statehood referendum would reverse the causality—instead of a white settler-colonial enterprise seizing power from native Puerto Ricans, in this case it would be Puerto Ricans themselves who make the final status determination. It would not erase the hundred-plus years of oppression visited upon the island by the United States, but it would certainly begin a process of recalibration through which the island's citizens can both prosper and thrive in the U.S. economic context, as well as maintain their distinctive culture. And unlike native Hawaiians, who are isolated in the broader context of American society, Puerto Ricans will join a complex tapestry of Spanish-speaking minorities like Mexican-Americans, who have managed to retain elements of their cultures.

Collectively, statehood for D.C. and Puerto Rico would be a revolutionary development in U.S. politics. It would be a particularly transformative development for Latinos in the United States, confirming once and for all that "American" is not an ethnic designation but rather an idea, genuinely open to everyone. By embedding itself fully in the constitutional order, Puerto Rico could begin to address the island's economic liabilities and bring real improvement in everyday conditions to its citizens. Importantly, Puerto Ricans would finally have full equality before the law and the same opportunity to elect their national representatives as the rest of the country. And while the outcome of a statehood process would definitely not please everyone on the island, it would finally end the protracted, painful, and circular debate about final status. There is something to be said for certainty even if you don't get your preferred option. Statehood for D.C. would rectify one of the Constitution's oldest and most intractable mistakes by granting the District's residents full and equal representation and putting them on equal footing with other small states and their disproportionately powerful representatives in the Senate. The District's residents would gain the same right to pass legislation and control their budget as those enjoyed by the residents of every other state in the country. The Metro, that vital artery that makes everyday life in D.C. possible, could be revitalized and transformed by the addition of new capital from neighboring commuters. In the final tally, residents would be gaining much, much more than they would lose. Just by themselves, four Democratic senators from D.C. and Puerto Rico would have made it impossible for the GOP to proceed with debate on their mindless and cruel health care bill. Betsy DeVos would not be Secretary of Education. Mike Pence would have had to be quartered permanently outside the Senate floor in 2017 to break a tie on every single piece of important legislation. And instead of needing two pickups to retake the Senate in 2018, Democrats would, after the victory of Doug Jones over Roy Moore in the December 2017 Alabama Senate election, already control the chamber.

These are slam dunks. This is easy math. Democrats must move, quickly and aggressively, to admit D.C. and Puerto Rico as the fifty-first and fifty-second states of the union as soon as they recapture power. Democratic and progressive organizations need to get onboard and make statehood for Puerto Rico a serious part of their organizing and activism. But it's still not enough. To truly achieve parity in the Senate, Democrats have to think even bigger. Like, California big.

## SEVEN CALIFORNIAS

As units of the first truly federal political project in the history of the world, the shapes of American states are largely happenstance, the result of settlers and entrepreneurs speeding across the new country, putting down stakes and then piling up enough citizens to move toward statehood. No thinking person would draw the boundaries of U.S. states as they currently exist, despite their colorful shapes and memorable zigzags. But perhaps no state other than Texas boasts the unplanned glory and nonsensical hugeness of California.

Prior to the Mexican-American War, California was a province of Mexico. Between 1822 and 1846, all the territories of what is now California, Nevada, and Utah, as well as parts of contemporary Wyoming, New Mexico, and Arizona, were administered by the Mexican government as "Alta California." The "Mexican Cession" granted all of this territory to the United States (although not Baja California). And long before it was stuffed with nearly 40 million seekers of sunshine, adventure, healing circles, and pot-limit hold 'em, California was the subject of nearly two hundred separate efforts to divide the state, most of them not particularly serious, but some no laughing matter. From the get-go there was turmoil over the size of the proposed new state, and its impact on the delicate compromise that allowed southern states to continue enslaving other human beings for economic gain without disrupting the union. And more than slavery divided the new territory. First, there was significant sentiment in Southern California for a separate state to avoid the destruction of Mexican-era landowners that was happening as industrialists and railroads gobbled up huge tracts of land in the north and as Congress forced people to prove their title to the land in court. New land use policies were particularly hard on Californians who predated the gold rush and the overnight population explosion of the early 1850s.[116]

In fact, in the 1850s alone, six different bills were introduced into the California state legislature seeking to create a separate state in southern California. In 1859, six southern counties voted to secede and form a separate state. As Kevin Starr, one of the state's preeminent historians, notes, "The outbreak of the Civil War scuttled separatist efforts in Washington, but the question of dividing California, while it has grown increasingly impractical over the years, has never fully gone away."[117] One of the more well-known outbreaks of California divisionism occurred in 1941, when a separatist "rebellion" broke out in four counties of Northern California, which styled themselves the state of Jefferson, sought to unify with several rural counties in southern Oregon, and went as far as choosing a governor and a flag, as well as erecting impromptu borders on highways. Separatist enthusiasts held an extravagant party to celebrate the new state on the fateful date of December 4, 1941. Three days later their dream would die along with thousands of their fellow Americans at Pearl Harbor. But the rebellion was probably never as serious or as widespread as it was made out to be in a series of sensationalist dispatches by *San Francisco Chronicle* reporter Stanton Delaplane, who actually helped stage the famous photo of separatists erecting a roadblock on Highway 99 and said in an interview decades later that he was functioning as the separatists' "press agent."[118] The spirit of Jefferson lives on today in Northern California's disaffected and downtrodden rural areas, where the state seal of mythical Jefferson is a popular t-shirt and flag design and where a small number of dogged separatists are still pursuing their impossible dream of separating a group of upstate rural counties from the rest of California.[119] The reason it is impossible is that it would create a Republican state with two new Republican senators. Doing so would require a vote of the Democratic-dominated California state legislature (and passage through Congress). This is not going to happen.

The state of California is so enormous that if you laid it out end to end, it would almost stretch across the entire black hole of empathy and human feeling at the center of the contemporary Republican Party. California alone is larger in land area than Germany, Japan, the Republic of Congo, and Vietnam, none of which are known as particularly compact and walkable places. Especially in the nineteenth century, governing such a large state from a single capital was a potentially insurmountable obstacle. You can see why the project is something of an inviting target. But more recently, the energy around a new division of California seems to have picked up some steam, most notoriously with venture capitalist Tim Draper's Six Californias initiative that very nearly made it onto the ballot for the 2016 elections. The beginning, middle, and end of Draper's vision for Six Californias was for the state's Twitterati and Googlarchs to have their own little archipelago of laissez-faire capitalism in San Francisco and San Jose, while the rest of the state is divided nonsensically into a series of farcical shapes and sizes. Like the mixed greens in a salad to the salad dressing, the other states of Draper's plan are just vehicles for the ambitions of the coders, angel investors, and app designers of Silicon Valley. Draper's plan has yet to attract the support of a single legislator or prominent politician in the state.[120]

Draper, however, may have accidentally stumbled onto the best idea the Democrats have to alter their structural disadvantage in the U.S. Senate.

In the past, breaking up California would almost certainly have produced several Republican-leaning states no matter how carefully you sliced it. The creation of Republican-leaning entities was clearly one of the signature intentions of Six Californias, beyond the selfish desire to hoover up all of Silicon Valley's prosperity for the benefit of America's tech overlords. But like the main character in *Office Space*, who tells his therapist that every day he wakes up is the worst day of his life, when the sun shines over the Golden State each day, it does so on the most left-wing moment it has ever experienced. The increasing leftward bent of the state of California means that, contrary to the situation even four years ago, there are a number of ways to divide the state that would ensure that all of the successor states are no worse than toss-ups for the Democrats.

The shift leftward has been less of a march and more of a warp-speed journey across the political galaxy. Once a reliable Republican stronghold, California went for the Republican nominee in nine of the ten presidential elections between 1952 and 1988.[121] In 1992, Bill Clinton won the state by nearly fourteen points over incumbent President George H.W. Bush, but Californians would send the anti-immigration zealot Pete Wilson back to the statehouse for a second term just two years later in 1994. The state remained in the ten- to thirteen-point range—still blowout territory but not exactly Vermont-style lopsidedness—until 2008, when things really started to go sideways there for the GOP. Barack Obama beat John McCain in California by twenty-four points in 2008 and Mitt Romney by almost twenty-three points in 2012 even as his margins were down in many other places in the country. Then in 2016, Hillary Clinton carried the state by an astonishing thirty points. You can see just how bad things have gotten for the GOP in California by looking at Orange County, the one-time conservative stronghold. In 1992, George H.W. Bush beat Bill Clinton in Orange County by almost thirteen points even as he was losing the state by thirteen.[122] In 1996, Dole bested Clinton there by almost fourteen points. When Hillary

Clinton carried Orange County in 2016 by 8.6 points, she was the first Democrat to win there since FDR in 1936. While the radioactivity of Donald Trump may have played a part, the county is at this point a tossup at worst for any generic Democratic presidential candidate.

The increasing progressive tilt of Orange County means that California could probably be divided into seven pieces, with all of them having a Democratic lean. Each of these seven new states would be centered around a major California metropolitan area and Hillary Clinton would have carried them all easily.

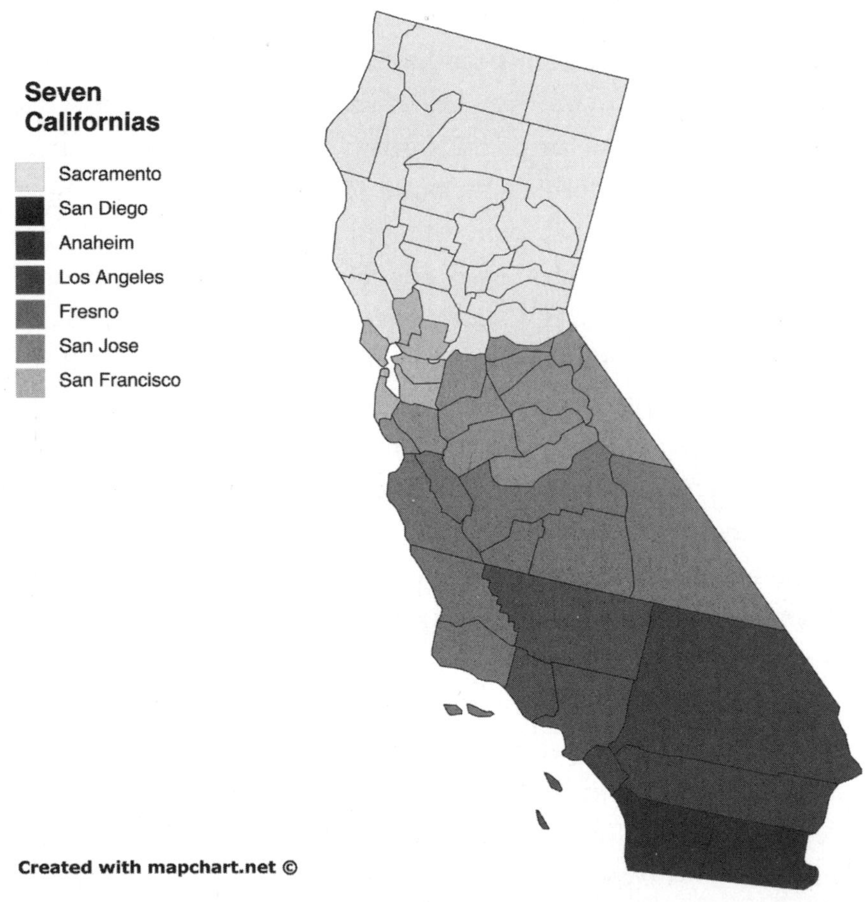

As you can see from this map, all seven entities would have access to their strange ocean, which is too cold for normal people to swim in. At the top would be the new state of Sacramento, including the rural, Republican-leaning counties of the state's northernmost expanses. Sacramento alone will provide the Democratic margins to ensure that it remains in the donkey's clutch. Just below it on the left will be the state of San Francisco, a compact, wealthy entity including Marin, San Mateo, Contra Costa, Napa, Solano, and Alameda counties. This state would be so Democratic it would have elected Hillary Clinton president even if she was caught hand-delivering satchels of uranium to Sergey Kislyak. The state of San Jose would be comprised of coastal Santa Cruz County and eleven additional counties stretching to the Nevada border. Democrats could run Colin Kaepernick for governor in this state and he would win by twenty points. The state of Fresno would include the coastal counties of Monterey, San Luis Obispo, and Santa Barbara as well as inland Fresno and four other counties to the Nevada border. Los Angeles would include Ventura, Los Angeles, and Kern counties, and would provide fake-election-in-a-dictatorship margins for Democrats. The state of Anaheim would be made up of Orange, San Bernardino, and Riverside Counties. Clinton would have carried this state easily by more than 211,000 votes despite the inclusion of traditionally Republican Orange County. Last but not least is the state of San Diego, comprising San Diego and Imperial Counties, another entity that would have gone for Clinton even if she had collapsed of exhaustion in a heap of classified e-mails documenting a torrid affair with Huma Abedin and forwarded carelessly to the president of the Iranian Revolutionary Guard Council. (Side note: deciding the fate of millions by drawing lines on a map is insanely fun! It isn't difficult to see why Europeans got attached to this practice as they invaded, extorted, and thieved their way around the world in twenty-seven decades. Oh, what did you do before dinner today?

Well I created a new country *with my pen* and this piece of dead tree flesh here. I'll leave it to you to decide who had the better day.)

Accomplishing a division of California would be by far the most difficult task of the ideas in this book for any group of newly ascendant Democrats. It would require a referendum (easy enough given California's bizzaro-world proposition system), an act of the California state legislature, and then an act of Congress. Californians take considerable pride in their state, and convincing them to cannibalize themselves would not be easy. There would be significant organizational, logistical, and financial challenges in setting up six new state capitals, dividing the state's debt, writing new state constitutions, and more. And no doubt, there would be even thornier issues, like figuring out who gets to keep which pieces of the state's sprawling university systems, crafting water-sharing agreements, and building a murder of gleaming new offices for the freshly minted state legislatures. It would require the kind of scratch that our elites generally reserve for invading small, unimportant countries, demolishing their societies, killing their leaders, and watching their young people grow up burning with a thirst for violent revenge against any American they can get their hands on. But ultimately the total cost of creating seven new states would probably be less than the price tag of some mid-range Pentagon boondoggle like the Osprey, and definitely far less than the amount of money Americans spend every year on Hulu subscriptions. If the cost of progress is a few new university campuses, some drab government buildings, and a bit of revenue sharing between California's successor states, then so be it.

It should, I hope, be clear why California must self-divide like some runaway cell. If the state were more or less evenly divided between left and right, its comparative lack of power in the federal government would be less of an issue. But California is now one of a handful of the most left-leaning states in the entire union, and Californians' lack of voting power and Senate representation means that the country is pulled inexorably to the right. In comparative perspective, California's shafting in the U.S. Senate is almost beyond belief. The United States is certainly not the only federal republic where the constituent units are wildly unequal in terms of population. But other countries at least take a stab at mitigating the inequality by awarding more seats in the upper legislative chamber to larger states. In Germany, the number of seats for the country's lander (states) ranges from three to six. While this still leaves some representational inequality in place, it is certainly a fairer arrangement than we have here. In the United States, we take it for granted that sparsely populated prairie states like Nebraska get to punch above their weight in electoral politics, while California, New York, Texas, and other larger-than-average states have to stifle their frustration by screaming into a pillow. Short of seceding from the union—something that is genuinely dubious constitutionally—Californians have no other feasible path to increasing their power without choosing to multiply and conquer. If Democrats had done this in 2009–2010, they would never have lost the Senate in 2014, would have been able to appoint Merrick Garland to the Supreme Court, and would currently be using their majority in the upper chamber to block President Trump and his Vichy Republicans from accomplishing a single thing in office. It wouldn't have prevented the Orange Menace from "winning" the 2016 election, but it certainly would have allowed Democrats to smother his presidency. Not only that but statehood for D.C. and Puerto Rico and a division of California into seven pieces would add twenty-two electoral votes to the Democratic column in most election years, which would have been enough to make Al Gore the president in 2000 and would make the Republican path through the electoral college even more difficult.

But subdividing would have benefits for California beyond simply increasing the state's power in D.C. First, it would offer a ladder to leadership for California politicians, who currently must bottle up 38 million people worth of national political talent in two senators, thirty-six congresscritters, and a governor. There would be seven governors instead of one Jerry Brown; fourteen senators instead of just Kamala Harris and Dianne Feinstein. There is also a solid argument to be made that states can be too large, and that Americans deserve some level of meaningful government beyond their own municipality to which they have actual access. Diffusing power out of Sacramento and into six new state capitals would perform precisely this service for all Californians. While it might seem like dividing the state would lead to economic inequality between the successor units—San Francisco the state would clearly be wealthier than Fresno the state—this is precisely why the division proposed here is careful to include a major city in each unit as well as access to the Pacific.

Could Republicans respond in kind the next time they are in power? The most probable candidate is Texas. The terms of the 1845 annexation appear to give Texas the right to divide into five pieces—four new states and a rump "Texas"—without Congressional approval. While there is heated debate about whether this is actually constitutional, and while it would likely be subject to vigorous litigation, the possibility can't be dismissed. The trouble for proponents of many Texases is that the state is no longer nearly as red as California is blue. When future prognostication superhero Nate Silver looked at the possibilities for Dallas's *D Magazine* in 2009, he showed that a division would create one overwhelmingly Democratic state, a swing state and perhaps three Republican states, based on the 2008 election results.[123] And that was with the 2008 numbers, which were considerably friendlier for Texas than the results of the 2016 election. But Texas has gotten substantially more liberal since then, and the overwhelming likelihood is that a divided Texas would be at best a wash for the GOP, due to the ongoing leftward march of major metropolitan areas like Dallas and Houston. George W. Bush carried Texas by nearly twenty-three points in 2004, but Trump took it by fewer than ten in 2016. Hillary

Clinton was the first Democrat to come within ten points of capturing the enormous electoral prize of Texas since Bill Clinton in 1996. As the state's heavily Latino population surges, the problem is likely to get worse, rather than better, for the contemporary GOP. While it might not be a true toss-up until 2024 or 2028, circumstances can change more quickly than we imagine. Remember, George W. Bush won solidly Republican Virginia by 8.2 points in 2004, only to see Barack Obama win it by 6.3 points in 2008, a 14.5-point swing in the space of a single presidential cycle. While Virginia was relatively close in 2016 due to the unexpected surge in the white vote for Donald Trump, it is generally regarded as a lost cause for the GOP for the foreseeable future. The nine-point blowout Democrat Ralph Northam inflicted on his Republican challenger Ed Gillespie in the 2017 gubernatorial race is further evidence of the state's leftward drift. Therefore, the worst-case scenario for Republicans would be that this maneuver might actually backfire completely, by creating more Democratic-leaning states, and thus senators. Other heavily Republican states, like Oklahoma, the Dakotas, South Carolina, and others, would either be too small to divide, or would clearly create a Democratic-leaning state in their wake.

Since his Six Californias initiative failed to make the ballot in 2016, Tim Draper has advanced a new proposal that would break California into three pieces. Unlike the first attempt, this would create three Democratic-leaning states and would likely send six Democratic senators to D.C. While the argument here is that California (and progressives) would be better off with the state in seven pieces rather than three, Democratic strategists should consider linking up with Draper on this proposal if they decide that a more radical division of California is too heavy a lift, or that voters might be confused by the appearance of multiple division proposals in the same election cycle.[124] What Californians must not do is to take seriously the effort to hive California off as a separate country. That proposal, known colloquially as Calexit, is almost certainly unconstitutional.

Worse, it would cripple the Democratic Party in what remains of the United States, making it nearly impossible for Democrats to capture the U.S. House of Representatives, digging the party a deep hole in the electoral college, and make it even harder to hold the Senate.

Let's not do that.

Collectively, this will be a heavy lift for Democratic policymakers. Welcoming eight new states to the union will require an enormous cadre of dedicated public servants willing to do the difficult work of sorting out the fiscal and logistical challenges inherent in creating new sovereignties. But imagine, for a moment, what is going to happen if progressives don't come up with some big ideas for the Senate. In the first year of the Trump presidency, progressives took great pleasure in watching GOP leadership fail to bridge the divide between its most liberal Senator (Susan Collins) and its most conservative (Utah's Mike Lee, one of the most right-wing individuals ever to hold national office in the United States). Paul Ryan and Mitch McConnell were so dreadful at unifying their rowdy caucuses that GovTrack, an organization that compiles all legislation in both chambers at varying levels of development, was incredibly pessemistic about the ability of Congress to make law. As of mid-October 2017, the House had passed 306 bills that were awaiting passage in the Senate, and GovTrack gave just 43 of them a better than 50 percent chance of passing the Senate and arriving on President Trump's desk for a signature. Despite the passage of the GOP's detested tax reform bill in December, most of these big wins are things like renaming post offices and federal research centers, and not a single one of the bills given good odds of passing represents a major plank in the Republican policy platform. If that pace holds up, Trump will have presided over one of the least productive Congresses since the thirty-second, which forwarded only seventy-four bills that were signed by the president. But one of the biggest thorns in the side of Senate leadership is Susan Collins of Maine, a state that will likely elect a Democrat or an independent to the office if Collins retires. Since the turn of the century it has become increasingly rare for anyone to hold Senate seats in hostile partisan territory for long. Those seats are generally won in wave election years, like former Republican Illinois Senator Mark Kirk, who captured his seat in 2010, or when the opposition makes some kind of calamitous error, as in 2012, when Indiana Democrat Joe Donnelly beat the hapless Republican nominee, Richard Mourdock, after the latter claimed that a woman impregnanted after rape is "something that God intended." Donnelly begins the 2018 election cycle as perhaps the most vulnerable Democrat in a state that Donald Trump won by nearly twenty points. As of this writing, ten Democrats hold Senate seats in states won by Donald Trump. Granted, some of them, like Michigan's two Dems, are in states that went very narrowly for Genghis Con. But the numbers are stark. Cory Gardner (R-CO) and Dean Heller (R-NV) are the only Senate Republicans up for reelection in 2018 in states won by Hillary Clinton. Because there are more Republican-leaning states than Democratic-leaning states, if the process of sorting out continues to its inevitable endpoint, it will be difficult for Democrats to ever capture the U.S. Senate absent a massive partisan wave. This will be particularly true if Republicans continue to make gains in Michigan, Wisconsin, and Pennsylvania, where Trump won, and places like Minnesota, where he came closer than is commonly realized because Democrats had bigger problems to worry about. But Clinton won Minnesota by fewer than 44,000 votes.

Trump won thirty states and Clinton won twenty. There are certainly cases to be made that some Trump states, like Texas, Georgia, and Arizona, are trending Democratic, but the reverse is true as well. Future Republican Congresses are likely to be even more radical, as the remaining moderates like Collins retire or are replaced by reactionaries via the primary process. At the moment it looks like the worst instincts of the Ted Cruz wing are going to be frustrated during Trump's first two years in office, but there is no guarantee that this dynamic will hold in the future. If people like Lisa Murkowski (R-AK) and Shelley Moore Capito (R-WV) are replaced by more bloodthirsty wreckers of the welfare state, there is almost no limit to the kind of damage they might inflict on our society. And indeed, in October 2017, the president's former strategy advisor Stephen Bannon revealed plans to run unhinged primary challengers against more than a dozen sitting Republican senators, including Majority Leader Mitch McConnell. If such people get into office and replace the few remaining sane voices in the GOP, America is in deep trouble. For these reasons, if the Democrats retake the Senate in 2018 or 2020, it could be their last chance in a generation to address this structural deficit. If they do not do so by making Puerto Rico and D.C. states and then moving aggressively to divide California, they may find progressive dreams frustrated time and time again by a GOP-dominated Senate that slips into Democratic hands only when something truly terrible has happened at the behest of Republicans. That just isn't enough. Democrats need parity in the Senate, they must have it, and this is how they could get it.

But they shouldn't stop there.

★ 4 ★

# The Neutron Option for the Supreme Court

When President Obama nominated Merrick Garland to the Supreme Court, it was one of the saddest farces in living memory. Squinting into the March sunlight and flanked by Garland and Vice President Joe Biden, a determined Obama, after a long, laudatory introduction of his nominee, insisted that he had the right to nominate a justice. It was, surely, the first time that a president nominated a justice to the Court knowing that he would almost certainly never be seated. "To suggest that someone as qualified and respected as Merrick Garland doesn't even deserve a hearing, let alone an up or down vote, to join an institution as important as our Supreme Court, when two-thirds of Americans believe otherwise—that would be unprecedented," he said. Garland himself, a mild-mannered, soft-spoken man, choked up when talking about the honor. Maybe he knew what was going to happen to him? Afterward, Senate Majority Leader Mitch McConnell remarked, bizarrely, that "It seems clear that President Obama made this nomination, not with the intent of seeing the nominee confirmed, but in order to politicize it for purposes of the election."[125] The idea that nominating a justice to the Supreme Court, a power clearly reserved for presidents by the Constitution, is an act of "politicization" represented a novel reading of both politics and the Constitution itself. But McConnell's naked cynicism had become routine during the most bitter fight over a Supreme Court nomination since the circus-like confirmation hearings for Clarence Thomas in 1991. Obama, in fact, had defied the left flank of his own coalition, which wanted a much more radical nominee, preferably a woman of color, to nominate Garland to the Court, hoping that a man who was profoundly uncontroversial in normal times might put enough political pressure on the GOP to force them to confirm. But Obama's fig leaf was offered to a Republican Party that had changed irrevocably in the past thirty years. Consider this: When Bill Clinton nominated Ruth Bader Ginsburg to the Supreme Court in 1993, she was confirmed 96–3. Just twenty-three years later, Garland, a man clearly to Ginsburg's right, couldn't even get a hearing.

Obama's Olive Garland would, of course, be viciously swatted away, as McConnell and his Senate allies closed ranks and made a stunning gamble—that the Republican nominee for President would win the election, at a time when that person was almost certainly going to be Donald Trump, and then fill Scalia's seat with another originalist. In February 2016, likely Democratic nominee Hillary Clinton frequently led Trump in hypothetical matchups by double digits.[126] And as the summer stretched into the fall, with Clinton holding her lead over Trump for nearly every single day of the campaign, Republicans started to make noises that if they held the Senate but lost the presidency, they would refuse to allow Clinton to fill the seat at all. Republican Senator Ted Cruz, in fact, had mused openly about how the ninth seat was unnecessary, and that Republicans might be happy to watch the Court shrink under a Clinton presidency as old justice after old justice died or retired. This is precisely the attitude that you can expect the Republican Party to adopt toward the Court should liberals ever succeed in restoring their first majority since the 1970s.

It is a bit of a cliché to wonder what future historians will make of the present. After all, the academic field of history is struggling to attract college majors, and many university presidents and provosts are busy sidelining this most vital area of human inquiry in favor of the STEM fields. But those clichéd future historians (assuming there is a future for historians to exist in, which requires the present to turn into the past, which requires someone other than Donald Trump to be elected president in 2020) will almost certainly write about Mitch McConnell the way today's scholars write about Joseph McCarthy and Andrew Johnson—as dangerous scoundrels whose machinations imperiled both the American democratic experiment as well as vital civil rights for millions of people. More than anyone alive, Kentucky's dollar-store Machiavelli has destroyed what little remains of Senate tradition, bipartisanship, and the idea that our elected officials will work for the common good and respect at least a handful of core democratic principles even while engaging in spirited partisan combat. With his signature dead-eyed, off-center stare, and his trash-eating half-grin that barely conceals his self-satisfaction with all of the democracy-wrecking shenanigans he's gotten away with, McConnell is the chief philosopher-king of the Republic of Hypocrisy, whose unrivaled ability to summon an unbroken string of lies, distortions, and self-serving nonsense through his teeth helped deliver unfettered power to the GOP in 2016 despite their almost unique unfitness to run a modern country.

But you know what? McConnell may have unintentionally done us all a favor by revealing that the reverence for the Supreme Court as an apolitical institution, resting nobly beyond the reach of polluted politics, is a charade. While the Court is still held in higher esteem than other branches of the U.S. government,[127] its public standing has been slipping as Americans realize that the two parties are treating it as an extension of the bloody-knuckle competition that has characterized national politics since the early 1990s. In fact, the crisis of the Supreme Court may finally lead us to understand that key features of how we operate the third branch of our Republic are kind of demented. The system of lifetime tenure that grants justices the right to sit on the Court until their grandchildren have grandchildren has created a crippling set of incentives for our political leaders and for the chamber itself. Elderly justices grasp their posts into their eighties or nineties, the average tenure of justices has exploded, and one of the central problems that early skeptics of judicial supremacy feared—that the Court would fail to reflect changing political times—has become a reality. And with the ascendance of Republican radicals in the early 1990s, the Court became what it had often been during the nineteenth century—a site of extraordinarily ruthless competition between partisans who understood full well the impact of controlling the Court and who had no shame about using procedural warfare to get their way. When McConnell, John McCain, Ted Cruz, and other Senate Republicans both prevented Obama from filling a vacancy and blue-skied possibilities for indefinitely preventing Hillary Clinton from filling the seat, they unwittingly opened the door for a radical overhaul of the Court by their opponents.

The theft of Merrick Garland's Supreme Court seat was an unprecedented act of democratic sabotage. The man who received the stolen goods, a statuesque zealot named Neil Gorsuch, was and remains illegitimate. And the only way for Democrats to regain control of the Supreme Court, and to precipitate a crisis that might usher in permanent reform, is to try to expand the number of seats at the earliest possible opportunity. As with so many other proposals detailed in this book, all it would take is a simple act of Congress, duly signed by the president, to increase the number of SCOTUS chairs. It was done repeatedly in the distant past, there is absolutely no constitutional barrier to doing so, and it could be done fairly easily in the present. The only thing preventing the parties from pursuing what you might call the Neutron Option is that for most of the modern history of the country, the two parties developed a norm that presidents should get to nominate whoever they like, within reason. And indeed, since the turn of the twentieth century, the scuttling of Supreme Court nominees has become increasingly rare, a tactic used only to block the truly corrupt nominees (as when

LBJ tried to elevate Abe Fortas to Chief Justice in 1968), the gravely unqualified (Harriett Miers, nominated by George W. Bush), or those whose ideology is seen as truly beyond the pale, and whose presence on the Court would drastically alter its ideological makeup (Robert Bork, a Reagan nominee who was spiked by the Senate). Because of this unspoken agreement between the two parties, both sides regarded Supreme Court openings as what they are—lotteries to be won by lucky presidents, or lost by those unfortunate enough not to preside over an opening. Ronald Reagan appointed three justices; Carter appointed zero. Bill Clinton, George W. Bush, and Barack Obama had appointed two prior to the death of Scalia.

The GOP's treatment of Merrick Garland means that this informal agreement is trashed. You could, theoretically, try to fish it out of the dumpster, uncrumple it, and try to convince everyone that it is back in force, but no one is likely to believe it. Here is a cold reality of politics in the twenty-first century, post-Garland: for the foreseeable future, presidents will never again get to fill a Supreme Court seat when the Senate is controlled by the opposing party. For Democrats, the next Republican president to face a hostile Senate should get nothing—no lower-court justices and no Supreme Court picks. This will remain true even in 2040, when Garland himself might be long dead. In the meantime, they should start preparing for an assault on the Republican Court majority that will allow them to withstand constitutional challenges to other recommendations in this book, as well as to push through a genuinely radical progressive policy platform. Democrats should also introduce a constitutional amendment to end lifetime tenure, as well as legislation, detailed later, to guarantee each president two seats on the Court. And yeah, that's probably not going to happen. So the centerpiece of the judicial counterrevolution must be an expansion. Democrats will have to plunge the knife in and twist it. Wouldn't doing so tear the country apart?

Most Americans surely remember, if only dimly from some high school history lecture, Franklin Delano Roosevelt's court-packing scheme from 1937. Frustrated by the Court's repeated decisions that struck down various pieces of his New Deal, FDR was increasingly anxious to put the Court in its place. He had been reelected in 1936 with one of the most overwhelming landslides in American history, bouncing GOP nominee Alf Landon by 24 points and carrying 46 out of 48 states. FDR's Democrats also swept back into power with a 49-seat majority in the Senate and a 246-seat majority (that's the *margin*, not the number of seats) in Congress, partisan dominance that is literally unimaginable in today's polarized climate. Legislatively, his party could do whatever it wanted. In fact, Democrats had so much power at the time, including control of state legislatures, that some believed they could amend the Constitution at will. The position of the Democratic Party in 1937 is something that devoted partisans spend their entire lives dreaming about but never seeing, like watching your favorite baseball team win 115 games and breeze through the postseason without ever losing a single contest. So why did FDR feel the need to launch a frontal assault on the Supreme Court?

His attempt to pack the Supreme Court is generally one of a handful of criticisms of FDR that transcends the left-right political divide, along with his internment of Japanese citizens during WWII (the Michelle Malkin wing of the right-wing fever swamp notwithstanding[128]). When he took office in 1933, the United States was in the throes of the worst economic crisis in its history, the gravity of which is difficult to convey to contemporary audiences unaccustomed to suffering on such a scale. The country's GDP had fallen in half between 1929 and 1933 and 13 million Americans were out of work,[129] with unemployment topping 25 percent. To appreciate the depth of this calamity, remember that the unemployment rate during the Great Recession peaked at 10 percent in October 2009 before beginning a long march downward to under 5 percent by the time the 2016 national election took place. A 10 percent rate of joblessness is an enormous national problem, but other societies, particularly those in Europe, have been able to withstand higher unemployment rates for extended periods of time without falling to pieces. But a 25 percent unemployment rate is a different creature: it is a crisis of capitalism itself and a national catastrophe, wiping out the future economic prospects of an entire generation of working-age adults. And because the unemployment rate remained at a staggeringly high 15 percent by the time FDR's second term commenced, the sense of national emergency was anything but diminished.

With America still scuffling along, and with his newly ascendant and overwhelming political coalition, the president decided to take aim at the one institution that stood between him and a total transformation of the political and economic system: the Supreme Court. The Court was stocked with conservatives, appointed almost exclusively by Republican presidents. When FDR took office in 1933, the country had been ruled by Republicans almost without interruption since the conclusion of the Civil War. On the Court that FDR originally confronted, only Louis Brandeis and James McReynolds had been appointed by a Democratic administration—that of Woodrow Wilson, who owed his election to the infamous split in the Republican ranks precipitated by Theodore Roosevelt's 1912 Bull Moose campaign. And McReynolds was no liberal—in fact he was counted by the administration and the press as one of the so-called "Four Horsemen" on the Court determined to snuff out the New Deal before it could take full effect. There was even still one William Taft appointee on the Court (Taft served as president from 1909–1913)—Willis Van Devanter. Two picks from Republican Warren Harding, one from Republican Calvin Coolidge, and no fewer than three justices appointed by Republican Herbert Hoover rounded out that Court.

The key here is that FDR faced the same hostile constellation of justices on the Court that the next Democratic president is likely to face. And so it is very important to understand why FDR did what he did and why his effort failed. During the president's first term, the Court had struck down a number of acts of Congress and key planks of the New Deal, including the National Recovery Administration (NRA) and the Agricultural Adjustment Act (AAA). FDR had grown tired of SCOTUS slapping down critical elements of the New Deal, and unlike most presidents who also despair of the Court's interference with their core agenda, he resolved to do something about it. The overarching fear was that the conservative majority would continue shredding important pieces of FDR's rescue plan, particularly the new old-age pension scheme known as Social Security. Perhaps most frustrating of all for FDR is that while three vacancies opened up during Herbert Hoover's single four-year term in office, not one seat had opened up between 1933 and 1937, which made FDR at the time the first president in the history of the Republic not to get to appoint at least one Supreme Court justice (he would later be joined by Jimmy Carter). Therefore, armed with a mandate and years of accumulated frustration with the Court, FDR worked in secret on a plan for stealth enlargement of the Court, which was then introduced into Congress. The bill would have allowed the president to appoint an additional justice to the Court for every sitting justice who did not retire six months past their seventieth birthday. Given the Court's makeup at the time, this scheme would have allowed FDR to appoint six new justices to the Court, giving it, at last, a liberal majority committed to upholding the New Deal.

His plan to expand the court to fifteen members, though, came to ruin and is almost universally regarded in political circles as an affront to democratic decency, in part because the Court is still held in much higher esteem by the American people than other political institutions. This is because no matter who you are, you probably have a hero there. The left has created the cult of Ruth Bader Ginsburg, while conservatives revered Scalia and, to a lesser extent, Samuel Alito. If you own "Notorious RBG" paraphernalia, you've engaged in this relatively harmless behavior. The image of the Supreme Court as a debating society protected from the ugliness of U.S. politics by a *cordon sanitaire* of nobility and higher purpose is broadly shared, if not as much as it once was. It is also total nonsense. While liberals and progressives may still have some residual affinity for the Court because of decisions by the Warren Court like *Brown*, the Court has been a bastion of conservatism for nearly the entire history of the United States. As James MacGregor Burns noted, "for much of its history, the Supreme Court has more often been indifferent to the wants and needs of the great majority of Americans."[130]

The federal judiciary has taken on a much broader role in American politics than the Framers intended shortly after the birth of the new republic. When Chief Justice John Marshall ruled on *Marbury v. Madison*, he established the principle of judicial review—meaning the ability of the Court to invalidate state and federal laws as being in violation of the Constitution. One of the most remarkable things about the history of the United States is not just that this arrangement came into being in the first place, but that it has been so rarely challenged by the political leaders who have often had to abide by Court rulings striking down key pieces of their agendas. Yet political leaders have frequently toyed with the structure of the Supreme Court to frustrate their opponents. One of the most notorious acts of political interference with the Court was the decision of congressional Republicans to reduce the size of the Supreme Court from nine to seven justices after Andrew Johnson—who they rightly regarded as an enemy of the project of Reconstruction—succeeded Abraham Lincoln as president of the United States. Lest there was any doubt about the purpose of this maneuver, they quickly restored the number of justices to nine when Republican Ulysses S. Grant was elected president in 1868.[131]

Even before Republicans destroyed the fairy tale of America's nonpartisan, apolitical Supreme Court by refusing to confirm Merrick Garland, the Supreme Court suffered from another of the

Constitution's design flaws: All justices in the federal judiciary are granted the right to stay in their offices if they so choose until they are carried out of them feet first. Perhaps lifetime tenure made sense when the Constitution was drafted, when the average life expectancy was probably thirty-five years or so, and even someone lucky enough to make it to fifty or sixty probably couldn't expect to live much more than another decade. Back in what the comedian Sarah Silverman once called "the olden-timey days," your life could end as the result of what today is a routine infection—strep throat, or the flu. Early American death panels were called doctor's offices. Today, men who successfully cross the threshold of age sixty-five are likely to make it past eighty-four, and women past eighty-six.[132] The signature challenge for most middle-aged Americans is how to care for their elderly parents, with dementia and Alzheimer's a particularly vexing problem.

You can think of the oldest members of the federal court system as America's declining parents. Instead of trying to get them to stop driving a car or move to a single-story house, we're just waiting for them to stop working and brush up on their golf games. Today, Ruth Bader Ginsburg and Anthony Kennedy are well past their eightieth birthdays, with Stephen Breyer approaching his, and Clarence Thomas nearing seventy. Most justices slow down and become less effective on the bench as they get older. According to Jeffrey Toobin, in the latter years of his tenure, Chief Justice William Rehnquist's "opinions shrank" in size and scope and he more or less abandoned any effort to persuade his fellow justices of anything. As Toobin notes, "fatigue was a factor too."[133]

The late Branch Rickey, the Brooklyn Dodgers general manager responsible for breaking baseball's racial apartheid system in the 1940s, once famously said about letting aging players move on to other teams, "Better a year too early than a year too late." America's judicial system keeps people years too late. Political research suggests that justices hang onto their offices far too long, hoping to retire under political circumstances that would allow them to be replaced with an ideologically similar person. Others just dig working. The length of tenure on the Court has skyrocketed over the years—justices who have retired since 1970 have spent more than twenty-six years in their seats, a number that used to be less than fifteen.[134] In many cases, the quality of their jurisprudence declines substantially in the process. Not only that, but justices serving short terms on the U.S. Supreme Court have completely disappeared in the modern age. Once a routine feature of the Court, the occasional justice serving a relatively brief term allowed the Supreme Court to be more responsive to changes in public opinion and evolving interpretations of constitutional doctrine. For instance, Eisenhower appointee Charles Evans Whitaker held his seat for just over five years before stepping aside in 1962. This no longer happens. Since 1970, no justice appointed to the Court has served fewer than eight years.[135]

Presidents have increasingly decided to take advantage of lifetime tenure to appoint younger and younger justices. These legal Doogie Howsers can then spend the rest of their long lives on the Court, long after that president has left office. Clarence Thomas was just forty-three years old when he white-knuckled his confirmation hearings and won a close 52–48 vote in the Senate. The Bush Administration was so desperate to have him sworn in before reporters confirmed key elements of Anita Hill's testimony about how Thomas harassed her that they rushed his ceremony. He's now been staring up at the ceiling in silence during oral arguments for twenty-six years, with no conceivable end in sight. As of this writing, Anthony Kennedy has been on the Supreme Court since 1987, before more than 124 million Americans were even born. Newly appointed originalist Neil Gorsuch was forty-nine when he was confirmed. Honestly: he looks like a healthy person. He could be on the Court until today's graduating college seniors are nearing retirement. If today's older conservative judges—Kennedy and

Thomas—are clever, they'll retire during Trump's first term, allowing the appointment of two more baby-faced ideologues and making it possible that a Democratic president will never ever get to replace a conservative on the Court.

As in so many other ways, the United States is an outlier among advanced democratic societies with these practices. And there are plans out there to address them.

## THE PATH FORWARD

A thirty-five-year-old graduate of the Medill School of Journalism, Gabe Roth started an organization called Fix the Court just four years ago, in the wake of a coalition he ran designed to foster greater transparency for SCOTUS. I met Roth in downtown Chicago at a place called Cafe Meli in July 2016 to talk about his group's plan for how to rescue the United States from the judicial wars. Over a breezy brunch, Roth filled me in on some of the details of the group's proposal, which he insists will (probably) not actually require a constitutional amendment. The law Roth recommends is not based on age, as FDR's was. It simply mandates that a president gets to appoint a new justice to the Supreme Court every other year. "Basically you'd have every odd numbered year, you'd add a justice to the court," he says. SCOTUS justices would be term-limited at eighteen years, and presidents would get to appoint a new justice in the first and third years of their terms.[136] This removes the element of random chance from Supreme Court appointments, routinizing them so that they are part of the normal political process. What happens to the judges who step down? Doesn't the Constitution guarantee them lifetime tenure on the courts? Rather than retire, the displaced senior SCOTUS member would, Roth's group puts it, "continue as fully compensated senior justices able to fill in on the high court following the death, retirement or removal of a justice."

They could also serve on lower courts, something known in the legal world as "riding circuit."

In terms of how the Court would function under this law, which Roth's organization has called the Regularization of Supreme Court Appointments Act,[137] the nine most junior justices would hear cases.[138] In the event of a Scalia-like sudden death, the most recently retired justice would be pulled back into service. Keeping senior justices in reserve may technically get around Article III's requirement that justices serve for life. Had this legislation been in place in 2016, Justice Stevens, who remarkably is still active and writing books, would have been pulled back into service, and then it would have been his court. This procedure also holds should the Senate decide not to confirm the president's nominee—the most recently retired justice would go back into active duty on the Court until the Senate confirms someone.

Roth argues that his law would bring with it a host of positive knock-on effects, including the phasing out of justices who are no longer fit for the bench. "If you look at the history of the court, every generation has had a justice who has theoretically had some mental health issues. So it solves an actuarial problem. Every decade past seventy you have a higher percentage of mental decline, whether dementia or Alzheimer's or whatever it is," he told me. Not only that, but it would encourage the appointment of *more* Merrick Garlands, people in their late fifties or early sixties who are currently eliminated from consideration because presidents are terrified that they won't serve long enough. "The idea that you can't have a (Richard) Posner, or on the right you can't have a (J. Harvie) Wilkinson because they are past their primes, is a problem." More experienced judges could be appointed to the Court, people in what Roth calls the "sweet spot" between youthful idealism and old-age curmudgeonliness.

The Fix the Court plan should be part of any Democratic push to reform the judiciary. First, Democrats must prepare—now—

signature-ready legislation to address the problem of the U.S. Supreme Court as their very first legislative priority in office. Here's how it will work. On day one of the 2021 Congress, presuming of course the Democrats have seized total control in Washington, the Democrats should introduce a constitutional amendment revoking lifetime tenure in the federal judiciary. The amendment should be offered up to the GOP as a grand compromise designed to bring the national judicial wars to an end. Unless there has been some massive political realignment in the interim, Republican minority leaders will instantly reject it. In today's polarized political environment, if a Democratic president believes the Constitution should be amended, there are twenty state governments that will oppose it no matter what.

What a constitutional amendment would do, instead, is offer the Democrats political cover for what I call the Neutron Option—the expansion of the Supreme Court to whatever number is necessary to secure a liberal majority. As soon as the GOP makes its opposition to an amendment clear, Democrats should move to step 2: increasing the statutory membership of the Court to eleven or thirteen (depending on how many justices President Trump ends up appointing). That legislation could be debated, enacted, and implemented within weeks of the inauguration of the next Democratic president, because there is nothing in the Constitution to prevent changes to the size of the Supreme Court. Finally, the party should introduce Roth's Fix the Court law (which also includes important reforms involving the transparency of Supreme Court judges, conflicts of interest, and more). The next Democratic president would thus (1) get to fill two or four new seats immediately, therefore flipping ideological control of the chamber and (2) proceed with the new plan of adding a new justice and phasing out an old one every other year. That plan, as Roth acknowledges, would be challenged in court as to its constitutionality. "In terms of the academic world, I'll readily admit that we're in the minority," Roth admits of the legal community's views on the need to amend the Constitution to impose judicial term limits.[139] That is why Democrats can't just rely on the Fix the Court plan, ingenious as it is. They must first pack the court, pressure the states and their GOP colleagues to amend the Constitution, *and* fight to ensure Roth's plan survives its court challenges. Ultimately, judicial term limits might end up being litigated before the Supreme Court, where a newly emboldened liberal majority can uphold it.

To understand how this would work in practice, let's do a little thought experiment: we'll assume that President Trump gets to replace Anthony Kennedy with, say, Diane Sykes of the 7th Circuit between now and 2020. That will preserve the conservative 5–4 majority when the Democrats ride into D.C. with total control in 2021. The Democrats then immediately expand the Court's membership to eleven and put Merrick Garland and Sri Srinivasan on the bench, giving liberals their long awaited majority, 6–5. Then Democrats pass the Fix the Court reform, granting the new president a third appointment, Patricia Millet. Because the Fix the Court proposal grandfathers in all existing justices under the old rules (i.e., no one appointed prior to the passage of the law can be forced out after eighteen years), this would temporarily put twelve justices on the Supreme Court. In 2023, the president will get his or her second regular appointment of the term. While the longest-serving justice would be encouraged to retire, theoretically both Thomas and Ginsburg could refuse and the Court would for a time have thirteen members. Wash, rinse, repeat. In the event that Garland, Srinivasan, and Millet are all still on the Court when their terms expire in 2039, one would retire immediately and be replaced by the president, while the other two would continue to serve until the next president makes his or her regular appointments in 2041 and 2043.

Finally, Democrats should, as one of their first acts in power, expand the number of judges in district and appellate courts in the

United States and fill those new vacancies with living constitutionalists committed to unraveling decades of originalist jurisprudence. Here again the right thing to do—relieving the extraordinary burden placed on the court system by Congress's inaction—lines up perfectly with the interests of the Democratic Party and the progressive movement. Judicial workload is a serious issue in many different courts in the federal system, and in bygone days (stop me if you've heard this before) Congress routinely increased the number of judges in the federal system, as well as the overall number of district and circuit courts. Congress has not seen fit to add circuits since the early 1980s, when it created the 11th Circuit by dividing the Fifth, and then in 1982 inaugurating the Federal Circuit.[140] And the number of judges has not increased significantly since 1990, when 70 million fewer Americans existed. In recommending passage of a 2013 bill to increase the number of judgeships in the circuit and appellate courts, Alicia Bannon of the Brennan Center For Justice argued that "the lack of federal judges over the last two decades has overburdened existing judges with unworkable caseloads, delaying justice to millions of Americans who rely on the courts to resolve their disputes."[141] As the *Huffington Post*'s Jennifer Bendery notes, since 1990 "there's been a 39 percent increase in filings at district and circuit courts but only a 4 percent increase in judgeships."[142] This creates unmanageable caseload problems for existing judges, and working conditions that make it hard to attract the best candidates.

Increasing the number of district and appellate court judges by about one-third should allow the next Democratic president to swiftly undo the damage caused by President Trump's appointing scores of unqualified goons and constitutional zealots to the courts. They will, unfortunately, be there for life, but if Democrats seize the opportunity to change the structure of the court system, they'll spend the rest of their miserable lives watching their opinions get reversed over and over again by liberal majorities at all levels. This plan will involve the creation of over two hundred new district judgeships and sixty appellate judgeships (if that seems like a lot of jobs to fill, the American Bar Association currently counts over 1.3 million lawyers in the United States.[143] We've got plenty.), something that might take years to actually carry out under existing Senate rules. But as noted in chapter two, the next Democratic Senate majority should simply change the chamber rules to approve large slates of judges at once. Like baseball managers who can ask for instant replay only on one or two plays a game, members of the minority or majority should be able to ask for short hearings on a limited number of particularly objectionable nominees without holding up the rest of the process. The remainder should be approved *en masse*.

If expanding the lower courts strikes you as an incendiary threat to the very idea of peaceful politics, keep in mind that such a plan is clearly under consideration on the right. Steven Calabresi, a Northwestern University law professor and one of the leading intellectuals in the originalist movement, published a paper with Shams Hirji in November 2017 recommending that while they hold Congress and the presidency, Republicans should immediately add 185 district court judgeships and 262 appellate court judgeships.[144] The first section of the paper is called "Undoing President Barack Obama's Judicial Legacy." You get the idea. While the Republican Senate as currently constituted is unlikely to entertain such a radical idea, you can be certain that future Republican Congresses will. It's only a matter of time. Remember: the current incarnation of the GOP is an antisystem party, committed neither to norms of judicial nominations nor to the baseline legitimacy of their Democratic opponents.

Democrats can make three primary arguments in this fight, which is likely to be uglier than a grammatical diagram of one of Trump's tweets. First and foremost is the treatment of Merrick Garland himself. Democrats can plausibly argue that not once in the modern history of the United States has an opposing party just straight up refused to confirm any nominee forwarded by a president. Yes, Robert Bork was prevented from taking a seat on the Supreme Court in 1987, but the reality is that Reagan was able to appoint someone to that seat in the end, which went to Anthony Kennedy. Holding Scalia's vacant seat open and then filling it with an originalist after Trump's fluke election victory therefore makes Gorsuch and his seat totally illegitimate from the get-go. That is the word Democrats should use and the strategy they should settle on to launch an all-out assault on Gorsuch.

Second, Democrats can make an even bolder argument: that no Supreme Court justice nominated by a president who loses the popular vote should ever be seated. By 2021, this will likely mean pursuing a campaign of delegitimization against Gorsuch as well as any other Trump nominees. (This will be moot if Democrats take the Senate in 2018 and no vacancies open up in between now and when the next Congress is seated.) The bottom line is that no justice appointed to the Supreme Court by Donald Trump should be considered legitimate. As impeachment is impossible under all but the most extreme wave election scenarios, Democrats must argue that they have no choice but to counter illegitimate appointments made by an illegitimate president with additional Court seats. Will the Democrats be accused of inventing a rule about Supreme Court appointments on the spot? Sure. But this is exactly what Republicans did when they claimed, preposterously and erroneously, that there was some kind of preexisting, bipartisan understanding that presidents don't get to fill seats during election years. Finally, just as GOP elites claimed, farcically, that they needed to shrink the D.C. Court of Appeals because it was underworked, Democrats can claim, with much more plausibility, that the Supreme Court needs the additional justices and clerks so that it can hear or at least sort through more of the thousands of cases appealed to it every year.

Such a plan would be less politically poisonous than you might think. Remember, first, that when asked by pollsters about it, a majority of Americans expressed their opposition to the Republican plan to stymie Merrick Garland's nomination. Democrats who hoped that the public would remember this affront to democracy in the voting booth ended up frustrated, because other considerations—the economy, immigration, terrorism, as well as the world-historical problem of Hillary Clinton's seven-year-old e-mails—turned out to be more important to voters when it actually came time to vote. In fact, spiking the Garland nomination was such a nonissue that it hardly registered in the 2016 election at all. If anything, McConnell and his allies may have correctly gambled that an open seat on the Supreme Court might convince traditional Republicans otherwise appalled by the behavior and personal history of Donald Trump to hold their nose and vote for him. Of the 21 percent of voters surveyed in the national exit poll who said that Supreme Court appointments were "the most important factor," Donald Trump won 56 percent to Hillary Clinton's 41 percent.[145]

Another benefit of pursuing a hard-knuckle scheme to enlarge the Court is that it could induce the next Democratic president's opposition to compromise. You don't need to look any further than the history of FDR's plan to see how this works. While history has mostly just recorded the failure of his effort in the short run (in the long run, of course, FDR completely remade American jurisprudence for a generation simply by winning four consecutive presidential elections), the official story conveniently overlooks the extent to which FDR's allies in Congress signaled that they might be willing to get behind a less severe version of his plan. Yet for some reason, the president decided that he would reject all of these overtures, believing that he had sufficient political capital to realize the maximal version of his plan.[146] In fact, the plan that FDR settled on was hardly the only option to challenge the Court that was on the table at the time. Some allies wanted FDR to push a constitutional amendment requiring a two-thirds Court majority to invalidate congressional statutes; some even more extreme versions would have granted Congress the right to override the Supreme Court's decision by passing the legislation again. While it is impossible to say for certain how such an amendment might have fared, some scholars believe that FDR could have made his achievements more permanent by deciding, as David Kyvig argued, to "write its view of federal obligation into the Constitution."[147] Members of the president's party in Congress were apparently willing to entertain versions of a court-packing plan that would have added fewer than five justices to the Court immediately, all of which the president rejected because he could not be certain that anything fewer than five would actually get him his New Deal majority in all cases.

The Democrats who pursue a court-packing plan should be prepared to withstand extraordinarily vitriolic attacks. But they should also be clear-eyed about what's coming at them in the long run from the Republican Party vis-a-vis the Supreme Court. GOP activists have long been livid that even a Court controlled by a majority of Republican appointees during the Obama Administration decided to side with the progressives at several critical junctures, including the gay marriage decision in *Obergefell v. Hodges* and the decision upholding critical pieces of the Affordable Care Act. Republican hostility to the role of the Supreme Court in American public life became so heated in recent years that party elites and activists talked openly of "shrinking" the Court by not filling seats.

This is almost certainly the strategy that would have been pursued by the party had Hillary Clinton won the presidency and Republicans held the Senate. "There is certainly long historical precedent for a Supreme Court with fewer justices," Senator Ted Cruz (R-TX) told reporters on the eve of the 2016 election. "That is a debate that we are going to have."[148] Extreme rhetoric coming from the most galactic jerk in the Senate is not surprising, but his threat was echoed almost immediately by Republicans previously thought to be in possession of cooler heads. Richard Burr (R-NC) told campaign volunteers that "If Hillary becomes president, I am going to do everything I can do to make sure four years from now, we still got an opening on the Supreme Court." And John McCain (R-AZ) joined in on the fun by saying, "I promise you that we will be united against any Supreme Court nominee [that] she would put up."[149] In normal times, these would be considered extraordinarily divisive, dangerous comments for politicians to make on the eve of their reelection campaigns. But these are not normal times.

If you've ever spent any time flying the USS Reality-Based Community through the asteroid belt of right-wing judicial thinking, you'll know that GOP activists have even more nefarious plans in mind than shrinking the hated Court. The Supreme Court and the lower federal courts are now certain to be the site of even uglier and more outrageous partisan warfare in the coming years. Conservatives have been itching to remake the Court, or to put it in its place, ever since a series of decisions in its liberal heyday, including *Brown*, *Miranda*, and *Roe*. In 2016, Josh Hammer, writing for Erick Erickson's influential reactionary website *The Resurgent*, argued that "It is also time for Congress to declare war on the federal judiciary." Hammer recommends "passing drastic jurisdiction-stripping legislation that deprives the federal courts of jurisdiction over entire areas of the law, such as abortion regulation or religious liberty" and believes that Congress has the power to "impeach federal judges for mere disagreement on the merits of judicial issues of great importance."[150] Taken together, Hammer's philosophy would amount to a three-pronged war on the judiciary: to strip it of its powers and jurisdiction, to shrink the federal and Supreme Courts, and to use congressional power to forcefully remove from office anyone that disagrees with the cultist interpretation of the Constitution.

Lest you think that these are merely the ravings of a random deplorable, these ideas all have the support of seemingly sane constitutional lawyers. Stripping the federal courts of their jurisdiction—that is, passing a law that says the federal judiciary may not interfere with state or federal laws on abortion, or gay marriage, for instance, is supported by a number of legal scholars. In the words of Julian Velasco,[151] "Like it or not, the courts must respect the fact that the Constitution has granted Congress nearly plenary authority to restrict federal court jurisdiction." Michael Stokes Paulsen, a law professor at the University of St. Thomas, recommended in an election-eve article for the *National Review* that "A statute shrinking the Court is an important symbolic reminder of Congress's various powers to check and balance an overactive federal judiciary."[152] Over the past forty years, ideas have had a habit of migrating from the right-wing fringe to the very center of Republican thought, and it can be expected that an all-out assault on the courts will eventually make its way into the laptop drafts of GOP speechwriters and parliamentary strategists, if for no other reason than the Constitution offers very little protection from it.

You don't have to look very far back in history to see how such a movement, while perhaps marginal today, could eventually succeed in destroying the entire federal judiciary as it is currently constituted. Having failed thus far to remake American society through the promotion of conservative justices through the ranks, the right will seek to sink the ship rather than capture it in a mutiny, and they will be able to do this because originalism is less a coherent judicial philosophy than it is a powerful social movement. As Robert Post and Reva Siegel argued, "The current ascendancy of originalism does not reflect the analytic force of its jurisprudence, but instead depends upon its capacity to fuse aroused citizens, government officials, and judges into a dynamic and broad-based political movement."[153] Democrats who believe that this movement will respect any existing norms about the federal courts are kidding themselves.

Beyond tinkering with the Court's size and jurisdictional powers looms an even more dangerous showdown: the very authority of the Supreme Court itself. The Framers did not intend to create a third branch of government with effective veto power over the legislature and executive. Indeed, the Court's powers and ultimate shape were not very well specified in the Constitution itself, because the document's architects could not agree on them. It did not establish the district and appellate court systems, but rather granted the power to create "such inferior courts as the Congress may from time to time ordain and establish." This is why Donald Trump's threat to break up or reorganize the 9th Circuit Court of Appeals in California is more than just empty rhetoric—it is, instead, the opening salvo in the right's coming war on the federal judiciary. After all, the right of the Supreme Court to invalidate laws duly passed by Congress and signed by the president appears nowhere in the Constitution itself.

The Court's power over the other branches of American government was, instead, created by *Marbury v. Madison*, a case whose importance was poorly understood at the time but that has been treated by nearly all successive generations as final. The case itself was insignificant on its own—outgoing President John Adams had appointed a man named William Marbury to be justice of the peace for Washington, D.C., but he had not yet taken office. Jefferson refused to seat him, and Marbury sued. John Marshall, the chief justice, ruled that while Marbury should be entitled to his position, the section of the 1789 Judiciary Act that granted SCOTUS original jurisdiction over the case (in other words, that it would go directly to the Supreme Court) was unconstitutional. Jefferson won his short-term victory—Marbury didn't get the job, and Jefferson's man did. But it established the principle of judicial review, by which the Supreme Court can invalidate laws passed by Congress and signed by the president as unconstitutional.[154]

There is absolutely nothing stopping a future Congress or president from ignoring *Marbury*. The deference of Congress and the president to the Court's rulings is a normative practice, albeit one supported by centuries of jurisprudence and state practice. America's reactionaries and conservatives have rarely called this overarching power into question because for most of its history the Supreme Court has been dominated by conservatives. With the exception of the Warren Court, it has not been controlled by liberals and jurists dedicated to expanding the scope of liberty and equality in American society for any significant period of time. In fact, the real test of the new right's commitment to judicial review will come only when a liberal Court begins striking down federal statute after federal statute passed by a Republican Congress and president. Eventually, the roulette wheel will land on that scenario, and you can bet your car that the reaction is going to be calling into question the very legal authority of the Supreme Court to strike down laws. In fact, abolishing judicial review altogether already has support from far-right legal thinkers, like the University of Texas law professor Lino Graglia. As he argues, "Because judicial review, much less judicial supremacy, is not explicitly provided for in the Constitution, however, an amendment should not be necessary. In theory at least, Congress could announce the view . . . that the Court's interpretation of the Constitution is not superior to that of Congress."[155] In other words, the next Republican governing majority to face a liberal Supreme Court majority may very well junk judicial review altogether.

Ultimately, the authority of the federal courts rests on normative practices and understandings. This is why everyone held their breath when the courts repeatedly struck down Trump's Muslim Ban early in his presidency. There is no magic dust in democracy, no *deus ex machina* to step in when one group of elites decides it is no longer bound by precedent and normative history. When customs agents apparently defied the court's orders in the first chaotic days after the ban was implemented, it raised the terrifying specter that the administration would simply ignore the authority of the appellate courts, and perhaps of the Supreme Court itself. The president himself impugned, with his trademark vulgarity, the legitimacy of the courts and of their judges. He is hardly the first president to rhetorically lay into the courts—calling them "unelected judges" is a staple of discourse for whichever group of people is currently dissatisfied by them—but he is the first president to combine delegitimizing rhetoric with a long history of remarks that call into question his commitment to democratic rule itself.

There is actually some irony here, because the wisdom of this arrangement, in the abstract, is certainly open to debate. No other country grants its high court this kind of sweeping power to overturn the will of duly-elected representatives of the people. But now that it has been in place for over 200 years, it would be extraordinarily disruptive to American society to diminish the authority of the federal courts, or to declare open season on judicial review. It is this path that Democrats must never go down, even when decisions go against them.

But even if Democrats win power in 2020, they might not be able to recapture the Court without winning two or three consecutive presidential elections and, of course, holding the Senate at the same time. Neil Gorsuch and whatever fresh-faced zealot replaces Anthony Kennedy are therefore the leading edge of a conservative plan to maintain the Republican Party's grip on American society even if voters reject them repeatedly. Yet a Court that strikes down a Medicare For All insurance system, or legislation establishing equal funding for public education, or that chips away at abortion rights, gay rights, and other issues that are now supported clearly by a majority of the public will create a profound crisis in American society of the likes that we haven't seen since the Great Depression. The best way to reduce the temperature around these battles, and to ensure that judicial review remains a broadly shared normative feature of American politics, is to eliminate lifetime tenure in the federal court system and to guarantee presidents one or two Supreme Court picks per term. If the reactionary right is unwilling to go along with this idea, as they almost certainly won't be due to short-term political calculations, Democrats must use the power granted to them by the Constitution to pack the Supreme Court, protect the legislation demanded by a majority of Americans and, hopefully, to convince their opponents that the current structure of the court system cries out for a bipartisan solution.

To help make sure a Republican majority doesn't replace the Democrats in the very next election and undo all of this progress, however, requires changing the way we vote for the House.

★ 5 ★

# Obliterating Winner-Take-All Elections

It is a blistering afternoon in a small office suite in the D.C. suburbs, and about twenty people are gathered to hear Drew Spencer Penrose, the legal director of an organization called Fair Vote, talk about the flaws in America's electoral system. The crowd is a mix of the organization's staff as well as a gaggle of fresh-faced interns, working for the summer for the seemingly quixotic cause of changing how America votes. Unlike places like the Brennan Center for Justice at New York University, which work on issues like voter access, Fair Vote is focused on changing the rules of elections themselves, rather than the struggle over who may vote in the first place. Spencer Penrose, a soft-spoken lawyer in his mid-thirties, first asks the crowd what our electoral system is even called. The question itself would strike most people who have not sat through a comparative politics seminar as bizarre. What is it called? It's called "democracy," dude! What are you even talking about? But a handful of interns do indeed know the answer—the United States uses a system called "Single Member District Plurality," or SMDP, for almost all federal legislative elections. Also known as "winner-take-all" or "First Past the Post,"[156] the U.S. system has a terrible reputation among the small circle of people who study the effects of electoral systems around the world. The one winner of each district's election goes to D.C. The loser goes home with some memories and a chance to live longer.[157]

The crowd is full of smart young people who really, really dislike this system. They pepper Spencer Penrose with questions about terminology and the effects of our electoral system. One gently corrects an error on one of the slides. Many of the interns are tasked with promoting an alternative to how the United States runs its congressional elections, called the Fair Representation Act. The FRA, which was introduced into the House in June 2017 by Rep. Don Beyer (D-VA), represents a fairly radical overhaul of the way we send representatives to Washington. Spencer Penrose himself, like many people his age, started paying attention to politics around the time of the 2000 election. The Nader campaign, which Spencer Penrose knew was doomed, piqued his interest in how America's winner-take-all system punishes smaller parties. Even if you make a big push for third parties, he says, "You'll very quickly run into winner take all as a problem."[158] Spencer Penrose went to law school at the University of Arizona (where he tried unsuccessfully to get the student government to change how its members were elected) and specialized in elections law.

Now he's got his sights on a bigger fish than the university legislature. He and his organization want to eliminate winner-take-all elections for the House of Representatives altogether.

But the United States should do more than just change how it votes. It should also make the House of Representatives significantly larger. In American politics, 435 is one of those numbers—like the 9 justices on the Supreme Court, the 100 members of the U.S. Senate, the 538 electors in the electoral college, and the zero operational neurons in Donald Trump's brain—that is presumed to be sacrosanct. Congress last voted to enlarge the House of Representatives in 1911, when it expanded from 394 members in the Sixty-second Congress to 433 members for the Sixty-third, with two additional seats set aside for the new states of New Mexico and Arizona when their statehood process was complete. It was the twenty-ninth time since the country's founding that the House had increased in size to keep up with America's growing population. Congress then passed the Permanent Apportionment Act in 1929, which capped the size of the House at 435, where it has remained ever since except for a brief period increase to 437 after Hawaii and Alaska were admitted to the union. This arbitrary number was selected almost solely due to fears that the House was becoming "unwieldy." But the population of the United States in 1930 was just over 123 million people. To say that the population growth of the second half of the twentieth century was unexpected is putting it lightly. Today, some 320 million citizens (we'll find out the exact number in a few years) share those 435 representatives. You have a better chance of sitting down next to Kanye at your local brunch spot than you do of accidentally running into your own representative, each of whom represents on average over 700,000 Americans. Those lucky enough to win a seat in the House spend an astonishing amount of their time dialing for dollars, rather than doing the difficult work of governing the country.

The size of the House is not the only thing that is completely out of whack about what the Framers intended to be the people's assembly. Every ten years, after the census, the district boundaries of every House seat are redrawn. Many states allow their own partisan legislatures to draw district boundaries, and those partisans rearrange the lines with Machiavellian zeal, seeking to trap their opponents in a small number of seats where they have an overwhelming advantage, and drawing the other districts so that they have a definitive, but not overwhelming, advantage in each of them, with the ideal being a 55–45 edge that can withstand all but the most towering electoral waves.[159] This process, known today as "gerrymandering," is one of the primary structural deficits of American democracy as it is practiced today. So many members of Congress are in "safe seats"—that is, seats that are reinforced to survive all but the most powerful election-day tsunamis—that barely a few dozen House seats are competitive in any given election cycle. While there is disagreement in the scholarly community about whether gerrymandering has contributed to the election of ever-more-extreme legislators,[160] it certainly hasn't helped. To this bizarre practice, the United States adds the most frequent legislative elections schedule in the entire democratic world, with every member of the House facing voters every two years, a truly bonkers practice that has created what critics call the "permanent campaign." It is the need to raise money every five minutes to fight for their own seats that has led to the dominance of fundraising in the job profiles of every member of Congress. The resulting chaos has contributed to the outrageous behavior of today's Republican Party in particular, with more and more extreme zealots with no real interest in governing or compromise ensconced in election-proof seats and loved by no one except (strangely) their own constituents.

After their overwhelming loss to the Democrats in the 2008 national elections, Republican strategists made the decision to focus their fundraising and electoral efforts on state legislatures and governorships in 2009 and 2010. Importantly, key elites were able to convince donors and fundraisers that the ratio of bang for buck was much higher in these races, which cost much less to run in the first place, than in national politics. The Republican State Leadership Committee raised $30 million for a program it called REDMAP (Redistricting Majority Plan) designed to flip control of state legislatures and governorships in anticipation of gerrymandering as many states as possible as far right as possible. In 2010, in addition to sweeping into the House of Representatives with a massive, sixty-three-seat gain, the GOP also captured nearly 700 seats in state legislatures across the country, including flipping control in Michigan, Pennsylvania, and North Carolina.[161] Republicans also flipped control of the governor's mansions in Florida, Iowa, Kansas, Maine, Michigan, New Mexico, Ohio, Oklahoma, Pennsylvania, Tennessee, Wisconsin, and Wyoming, an almost unbelievable bloodbath that, combined with GOP state legislative victories nationwide, left the party in almost total control of the redistricting process after the 2010 census. Republicans could draw 193 of the districts in the House by themselves, while Democrats had the ability to do so with only 44 seats.[162] Nonpartisan commissions controlled 88 seats, and 103 had to be drawn up by a combination of the two parties. What the GOP did with those 193 seats is two things: one, pack Democrats and their voters into a small number of overwhelmingly blue seats, particularly urban districts that Democrats will win by fifty points or more; and two, draw clever lines so that Republican candidates are fighting in districts where they have significant but not overwhelming natural advantages. David Daley, who authored the definitive account of this project, told me that due to sophisticated mapmaking software, "You can now draw districts that are 55–45 but that are not particularly vulnerable to a wave."[163]

The GOP's fiendishly clever REDMAP program after the 2010 midterms delivered the party eight years of uninterrupted rule in the House of Representatives from 2011 until at least January 2019. That plan was so successful that it even allowed the party to weather the loss of the national popular vote for the House in 2012 while still retaining a substantial seat majority. Republicans in the House began acting with the kind of arrogance and indifference to public opinion that can happen only when politicians know they can basically never lose a reelection race outside of a primary. The subsequent behavior of the Republican Party was such a horror show that Americans consistently gave Congress approval ratings below 20 percent. Yet the ingenious 2010 gerrymander combined with low Democratic turnout and a nadir in President Obama's approval rating helped Republicans hold the House decisively in 2014. And while some observers thought Democrats could retake the House in 2016, gerrymandering together with Hillary Clinton's unpopularity allowed the GOP to turn a narrow vote majority in House races into yet another overwhelming advantage. Unfortunately, the problem is much more complex than simply having the Democrats win power at the state level in 2019 and 2020 to perform their own gerrymandering for the next reapportionment. This is because Democrats and Republicans are not distributed evenly throughout the general population, but are instead increasingly concentrated together in their preferred locales. Known as "the big sort," it is less a conscious process where people search for places to live à la Richard Florida's "creative classes" and more of a sociological phenomenon where living in certain kinds of places over time tends to produce particular economic and political attitudes. As Daley explained to me, even if Democrats get to draw the district lines in more states after the next census, it probably still won't be enough to truly level the playing field. "It doesn't matter if Democrats get more votes. Everything is really stacked against progressives. Or we can use this moment to think seriously about our electoral system."[164]

Bill Bishop, who coined the term "big sort" argued that "we now live in a giant feedback loop, hearing our own thoughts about what's right and wrong bounced back to us by the television shows we watch, the newspapers and books we read, the blogs we visit online, the sermons we hear, and the neighborhoods we live in."[165] It's not necessarily the case that every Democrat in Illinois made a conscious decision to move to Chicago (although this does happen) as much as living in Chicago over time has tended to turn people into progressives with a fairly predictable set of underlying beliefs about the role of religion in government, U.S. immigration policies, and tax structures. This is not to say that progressive individuals don't sometimes make their life and career choices on that basis, just that intentional choice is probably not what is driving the long-term trend toward being surrounded exclusively by people who basically agree with you about everything. If you're like me, you might have moved to a city from the suburbs after college, not to purposively seek out exclusively left-wing neighbors but to attend graduate school or take a job. Over time, perhaps you found yourself increasingly incapable of understanding your counterparts in rural areas.

After the 2016 election, this trend was derisively referred to as a "liberal bubble" of fellow coastal-global-elitists who supposedly look down on the hayseeds in flyover country, attempt to police the etiquette and morals of rural folks, and seek to enforce their European vision of American society on an unwilling country. This sorting has dominated electoral trends since the turn of the century. In 2016, 90 percent of counties with fewer than 100,000 voted more heavily for Donald Trump than they did for George W. Bush's reelection in 2004.[166] On the flip side, in America's large metropolitan areas, those with more than 500,000 people, 82 percent voted more Democratic in 2016, often by substantial margins, than they did in 2004. As Damon Linker argued after the 2016 election, the "sociological core" of our polarization is "a growing socio-cultural chasm pitting the city and the countryside against each other."[167]

The lack of proportionality and fairness can seem more or less absurd depending on what state you look at. The state with perhaps the worst disjuncture between the expressed wishes of its citizens as measured by elections and its congressional delegation is Pennsylvania. The Keystone State is more or less evenly divided. Until 2016, it was thought to have a slight Democratic lean at the presidential level, but Republicans have frequently won the governorship as well as one of its two Senate seats. There are a million more registered Democrats in Pennsylvania than registered Republicans. Yet in this relatively balanced state, which Donald Trump carried by a margin thinner than his policy depth, the current House delegation is thirteen Republicans and five Democrats. You don't have to believe uncritically in simple majority rule to see that a party controlling 72 percent of the seats in a state in which it has, at best, 50 percent support is problematic. The issue is not restricted to evenly divided states, either. In Alabama, where Trump beat Clinton by more than twenty-seven points, there are six Republicans and just one Democrat in the delegation. In Missouri it's six Republicans and two Democrats in a state with, at worst, a 3 to 2 Republican lean.

In Nebraska, a state where Clinton pulled a third of the vote, there are zero Democrats out of three House members. In Connecticut and Massachusetts, there are no Republican representatives in the House out of fourteen total seats between the two states. While both are overwhelmingly Democratic states, it is also not right for one of the two major parties to be completely shut out.

David Daley notes that "America is the only major democracy in the world that allows politicians to pick their own voters."[168] If you put these two things together—the enormous power that partisans wield in the redistricting process, together with the tendency of committed partisans to live together and go weeks at a clip without running into a person who supports the party on the other side of the aisle—has created a unique dilemma for the Democratic Party. While gerrymandering gets its share of the blame, it often gets too much. The reality is that there is almost no way to draw district lines for a 435-person House without clustering Democrats together in a relatively small number of uncompetitive urban seats. Even if every state used independent or nonpartisan redistricting processes, like California or Iowa, such procedures "do little to resolve the partisan bias in House elections."[169] And even if Democrats capture such power in the next several cycles that they control the redistricting process in a majority of states, they will not be able to gerrymander their way out of their structural problems. And indeed, popular resentment against gerrymandering is growing and may prevent the party from engaging in district-drawing shenanigans without inviting a massive electoral backlash. Not only that, but the Supreme Court is set to rule on the gerrymandering of the Wisconsin legislature and may throw out the whole process of partisan gerrymandering altogether. While that is to be applauded, it points to the need for Democrats to consider a bolder solution: changing the way we vote for the House rather than tinkering with how the districts are drawn.

So if Democrats can't fix this problem by winning power and

returning the favor, is there a better plan? There are several possible ways out of the woods here. One is to simply replace America's system of "winner take all" elections for the House with some version of proportional representation (in which parties are awarded seats roughly in proportion to their percentage of the vote).

What's wrong with the Single Member District Plurality system we use in the United States? Before you bite down on your tongue to stay awake, stay with me for a minute, because using this system has important and poorly understood knock-on effects that structure our politics in a variety of important ways. Americans frequently complain about the two-party duopoly that has characterized national politics since the lead-up to the Civil War, when the Whig Party disappeared and the Republican Party rose to take its place. Almost no one is pleased by all the policy positions adopted by the leadership of their preferred party, because both parties are large coalitions of diverse interest and demographic groups. Because there is one and only one winner in each congressional district, the losers go home with nothing, and the system itself places near-insurmountable pressure on smaller parties seeking to break up the major party monopoly. You have a better chance of surviving a fall out of a tenth-story window than you do of winning a seat in the House without a (D) or an (R) next to your name. This hunch is confirmed by reams of scholarship in political science, showing that countries using our system have fewer significant political parties than countries employing proportional representation.

The tendency of our system—SMDP—to produce two major parties to the exclusion of most others is actually enshrined in one of the few reliable findings of modern political science and is known as "Duverger's Law."[170] Countries that use varieties of proportional representation (PR) have, on average, more significant political parties (i.e., parties that can be expected to win a substantial number of seats and thus participate in the formation of governing coalitions) than those that use SMDP.[171] To illustrate this point in our own system, imagine that the Green Party, for instance, tripled or quadrupled its vote share in the 2018 midterms, and consistently won 10 to 20 percent of the vote in most districts. (The Greens would need to clean the anti-vaxxers and GMO paranoiacs and chemtrails caucus out of the party for this to ever happen but whatever. This is a thought experiment.) Because we award power to the candidate with the most votes, even if that is less than a majority, those millions of votes would likely translate into precisely zero seats in the House, whereas in a system using PR, the Greens would be awarded a number of seats roughly proportional with their overall percentage of the vote. If seats were awarded based on the percentage of the vote, either nationally, by state, or even by larger districts, Republicans would probably hold three to four of the seats in the Massachusetts delegation, and Democrats would split the Pennsylvania House contingent evenly with Republicans.

Americans have consistently expressed support for having more realistic options than just Democrats or Republicans. Prior to the 2016 election, a Gallup poll found that an astonishing 57 percent of Americans wanted a third-party option to vote for.[172] While that number may have had something to do with widespread dissatisfaction with both major-party nominees in 2016, it also suggests that the desire for a third and fourth relevant political party is more widespread than is commonly understood. But it is also highly likely that instituting a system of proportional representation would scramble our politics in unforeseen ways. It is those unknown unknowns that make pursuing proportional representation a huge risk for Democrats. It might take several electoral cycles for the party system to congeal into some kind of rough shape. And it's important to keep in mind that proportional representation would enable gains for parties of the right beyond the Republicans, and that the map could be scrambled in strange ways—both the Republican and Democratic coalitions would almost certainly be broken up into at least two pieces. Republicans might fragment into two parties, with the remaining Rockefeller Republicans walking away with the rump GOP and the Freedom Caucus true believers forming their own hard-line constitutional party.

For the Democrats, the party would likely split into what you might think of as roughly the Clinton and Sanders wings of the party, although this is not always a productive way to think about intraparty struggles. But depending on where the threshold for gaining seats is set, you could see an even more significant fragmentation. In the Netherlands, where there is no meaningful threshold for parliamentary representation whatsoever, there are well over a dozen significant parties, with thirteen in the current body that was elected in March 2017. The Dutch parliamentary system is so fragmented that truly unique and marginal organizations have gained some power, including a group called The Party For Animals.

There are, however, some mid-range options between pure, continental-European style proportional representation and America's disastrous winner-take-all congressional elections, ones that would both significantly enlarge the House and lead to outcomes that more closely reflect the actual breakdown in votes between the two parties. And sorry, but this is another one where you might want to pop an Adderall and a Red Bull to follow along with me. The plan favored by Fair Vote, and which now has an actual bill in the House with actual sponsors, is known in political science circles as "the Single Transferable Vote" (STV). Aside from being a little too close to "STD" for comfort, the bill's proponents prefer to call it "ranked choice voting," or RCV. In this system, in most states, the districts will elect either three or five members, instead of just one as they do today. Voters will be able to rank-order those candidates rather than choosing one and only one. In RCV voting, the way it works is this: on the initial tally, the candidate with the lowest number of first-preference votes (i.e., the person ranked first by the fewest number of voters) is eliminated from the competition. However, those ballots are not dead; whoever is ranked second on those ballots gets that vote. So if I vote for Jill Stein and she is eliminated, my vote goes to whoever I ranked second. If we are further into the process and my second choice has also been eliminated, my vote goes to the person I ranked third. This process is repeated until all of the seats in the district have been filled. Does that sound complicated? It is. That's why the Fair Vote plan also includes money for all of the states to conduct voter education plans so that everyone understands what they are doing when they walk into the voting booth. There might be some hiccups the first few times, but other societies, including Ireland, have been able to institute this system without any real problems. You can see a sample ballot below.

| City Council - 3 to be elected | | | | | | |
|---|---|---|---|---|---|---|
| Rank up to 6 candidates.<br>Mark no more than 1 oval in each column. | First choice<br>1st | Second choice<br>2nd | Third choice<br>3rd | Fourth choice<br>4th | Fifth choice<br>5th | Sixth choice<br>6th |
| **Valarie Altman**<br>Orange Party | ⬭ | ⬭ | ⬭ | ⬭ | ⬭ | ⬭ |
| **George Hovis**<br>Yellow Party | ⬭ | ⬭ | ⬭ | ⬭ | ⬭ | ⬭ |
| **Althea Sharp**<br>Purple Party | ⬭ | ⬭ | ⬭ | ⬭ | ⬭ | ⬭ |
| **Mary Tawa**<br>Lime Party | ⬭ | ⬭ | ⬭ | ⬭ | ⬭ | ⬭ |
| **Joe Li**<br>Tan Party | ⬭ | ⬭ | ⬭ | ⬭ | ⬭ | ⬭ |
| **Phil Wilkie**<br>Independent | ⬭ | ⬭ | ⬭ | ⬭ | ⬭ | ⬭ |

The advantages of using this system are countless. To begin with, it would truly reduce the "incumbency advantage" that allows so many House members to cruise to reelection even if they've spent most of their time in office dialing for dollars, lunching with lobbyists, and grandstanding for the most committed partisans. As Spencer Penrose noted in his presentation, it also means that to run for Congress, you don't necessarily have to take the suicide plunge of running against a sitting member of the House—you're functionally running against anyone and everyone in the field. While parties would still hold primaries which would narrow the number of candidates down to the number of seats in the district, candidates would no longer need to mount a specific, frontal challenge against a sitting member of Congress in their own party. For instance, this year sitting Democratic Congressman Dan Lapinski of the third district in Illinois is being challenged in a March primary by non-profit leader Marie Newman. Under the Fair Representation Act, Newman would not have to run *specifically* against Lapinski, and parties would be less able to influence the direction of these primaries by protecting incumbents. While it wouldn't erase the incumbency advantage, in the long run this reform would open up political competition to hundreds of new challengers with new ideas about our politics. It would also deeply affect, in theory, the character of our winner-take-all elections. Candidates would be incentivized to seek votes beyond their own bases. Perhaps the Democratic candidates would be forced to appeal to more moderate Republicans to head off the challenge from parties further to the left. Or, alternately, Democrats might get pushed to the left so that they are ranked second by voters who prefer candidates from the Green Party or the Working Families Party. The precise dynamics can't be predicted in advance, but we can know with certainty that our stale politics would receive a jolt of energy and uncertainty.

The competition in each district might differ based on the ideological and demographic character of each place. The need to create majority-minority districts to elect African Americans or Latinos into office (i.e., districts deliberately drawn to hold a majority of minority voters so that a minority might actually get elected)—

something that actually helps conservatives by giving Republicans a greater advantage in other districts—will be gone. Most districts in this plan would have enough minority voters that minority candidates could gain representation even if white voters acted like an ethnic bloc and refused to cast ballots for them at all. It also makes gerrymandering a thing of the past—while the larger states would still have multiple districts, it would be almost impossible for the software wizards in each party to draw to their advantage. Fair Vote actually challenged one of their data magicians to draw the proposed district lines in Texas to maximize the GOP advantage, to little avail.

In the United States, this system would work a series of instantaneous miracles, nearly all of which would benefit Democrats and their progressive allies. First, it would allow voters to make both strategic and passionate choices at the same time. Instead of being forced to vote for Democratic candidates who don't necessarily share their values because the alternative is some Tea Party nutcase, citizens could vote with their hearts *and* their minds. They could cast a first-choice ballot for a Green Party or the Working Families Party candidate without fearing that they are tossing their ballot away, because even if that candidate doesn't get a seat, your second, third, or fourth choice votes will be redistributed to remaining candidates. Second, instituting this system would immediately demolish all incentives to gerrymander individual House districts, because the ultimate result will be much more proportional no matter what. Districts could be united by interest and shared community rather than drawn by diabolical mapmakers who create insane districts like the infamous "earmuffs" district in Illinois's fifth, which includes parts of north and south Chicago and then bizarrely juts out in a narrow loop through the suburbs and exurbs.

In fact, the FRA would more or less eliminate bloody, bruising gerrymandering battles from our national politics altogether. Although it would not be a panacea for the problem of increasing extremism in our politics, bringing new parties into the mix, and forcing the major parties to compete for all voters in every state, would certainly decrease the tendency of voters to return to office, election after election, hardened radicals who sleep peacefully at night knowing that only a one thousand-foot-tall partisan tsunami could ever sweep them out of office.

The United States also does have a history with the family of voting systems that the FRA would usher in. In 1870, Illinois changed its voting system for the state legislature to something called the "cumulative vote," a system that is now out of favor with democratic theorists and that allows voters in multimember districts (that is, a district that sends multiple representatives to the legislature, as opposed to our system, which sends one per district) to cast more than one vote for any single candidate, or to distribute them as they see fit. Illinois only repealed this system in 1980. During the 1800s, various proposals to reform the U.S. voting system were entertained only to be defeated or discarded.[173] But they serve as proof that it is possible to debate and implement major changes to how we elect our representatives. As Spencer Penrose told me, "Proportional Representation is part of the American experience. Over two hundred jurisdictions use some form of non-winner-take-all."[174] American voters in places like Minneapolis, Minnesota are able to participate in these kinds of systems without major problems.

The lone disadvantage is that of the world's major electoral systems, RCV is probably the least studied and understood, because it is used in so few places.[175] Political scientist Donald Horowitz claims that RCV produces "relatively proportional results," although the impact is better the more seats are contested in each district.[176] David Farrell, Jane Suiter, and Clodagh Harris make the important note that RCV is probably the least proportional of all systems that are considered a form of proportional representation.[177] And as the Irish experience indicates, lower district magnitudes (i.e., the number of seats in each constituency) are associated with less proportionality in election results.[178] It is also worth noting that there is significant dissatisfaction with the Irish system as it currently exists, with several major parties promising to replace it with another system prior to the 2011 elections.[179] But the advantages of instituting RCV in the United States far outweigh the disadvantages. The reform would lead to enhanced minority representation. As Drew Spencer and Rob Richie note, "choice voting would guarantee that every African American voter—in fact every voter, period—could point to an elected legislator that he or she helped elect."[180] RCV could limit the impact of the post-Citizens United deluge of billionaire scratch in our politics by making every race in the country a competitive one, and thereby depriving oligarchs and their associated SuperPacs of the opportunity to target their money at the small number of swing seats.[181] The reform would have to be carefully designed and studied, but the net impact would be positive, both for American democracy and for progressives.

Because there is a signature-ready bill in Congress, the view here is that Democrats should push the Fair Representation Act when they get back into power, with one important modification—the existing plan would keep the number of House representatives at 435. However, if paired with an enlargement of the House—I suggest a simple doubling to 870—the Fair Representation Act would transform our party system and increase Americans' access to their representatives and substantially increase the opportunity for new blood to get into the system. Importantly, it would also remedy one of the plan's most significant flaws—that district sizes of between three and five representatives are simply too small to rectify the absence of proportionality in the American party system. Studies have shown that with small district magnitudes, ranked choice voting does not create results that increase proportionality in results as much as larger districts do. And while an 870-member legislature will certainly be large by global standards, it is by no means absurd. The United Kingdom, with a fraction of America's population, elects a 650-member House of Commons. The European Union, an entity with a similar population to that of the United States, has 751 seats in its lower chamber. These legislatures function just fine. While the 10,000-member House needed to strictly comply with the Constitution's language about the constituent-to-legislator ratio is unrealistic, there is nothing other than a lack of imagination stopping the United States from significantly increasing the size of the House.

One of the primary objections to both changing the electoral system or enlarging the House is that the members of the House would never vote to dilute their own power. From a purely rational standpoint, it is better to be one of 435 than one of 870. Rightly sensing that a larger House might create more competition for advancement, spots on the top committees, and simply distinguishing oneself from the horde, members of the House would never voluntarily diminish their own influence. Yet the evidence against this claim is right there on the record of American history, and members of Congress proved their willingness to water down their power on twenty-nine separate occasions, back in the days when maintaining some fealty to the Constitution's language by increasing the number of representatives for a growing population was a commonly agreed-upon value. Democrats in particular also must feel the sting of being so long in the minority—it is harder to recruit good candidates for office or talk people out of retirement when the future looks bleak, and even those representatives who remain in Congress have low morale because they have no opportunity to do what they went to Washington to do, which is to make policy that impacts American society for the better. Recruitment problems for the Democrats left the party with an aging leadership for the 2016 elections, with few plausible candidates for national figures to emerge.[182] Anything that makes it more likely that House Democrats and their allies will be able to wield power for more than five minutes should be something that these leaders embrace as a long-term strategy for the progressive movement. After all, Democrats set aside their short-term interests to pass Obamacare in 2010—many leading House and Senate Democrats were obliterated in the 2010 Republican wave. They could be persuaded to do so again.

Enlarging the House would also pave the way for eliminating one of the most demoralizing aspects of our reapportionment process—stripping representatives away from states that have lost population. After every census since 1929, states have been deprived of their voting representatives in the House if they lost population or grew less quickly than some of their counterparts. In recent years, most of this movement has been away from the "Rust Belt" states in the Upper Midwest and the cold-weather states of the Northeast to the faster-growing parts of the country in the Southeast and West. Yanking representation away from states and citizens who have already suffered through economic dislocation is a particularly cruel act that only reinforces the sense of loss felt by voters who then have to watch their existing representatives fight it out for a diminished number of seats, a kind of political musical chairs that ends with members of the House losing their offices not because of poor performance or corruption but because their state has not attracted new citizens the way some others have. Reducing the constituent-to-legislator ratio would also make it more plausible to start talking about statehood for other U.S. overseas territories, including the Virgin Islands (population 103,574) and Guam (161,785), all of whom would presumably lean Democratic since the Republican Party has seemingly been captured by racist fanatics.

If all goes well, Democrats may be afforded an extremely rare opportunity after 2020 to fundamentally change the toxic environment in the House of Representatives. All they need to do is take the existing ideas that are out there and run with them. Doing so would be the most audacious and transformative attempt to change how we elect our representatives since citizens were granted the right to directly elect their own senators. The authors of such a reform would be remembered, fondly, by future generations for bequeathing a more noble, representative, and effective form of governance to future generations. Above all, they would finally overturn the effort of nineteenth-century political elites in the United States to, as Amel Ahmed puts it, "contain working class mobilization, and particularly, the rise of socialist parties with an agenda of radical social transformation"[183] by using America's system of winner-take-all election to exclude more radical challengers.

But there is one more thing Democrats must do to permanently alter our political trajectory: address the shameful and exclusionary voting practices that give America one of the lowest turnout rates in the developed world.

★ 6 ★

# The Modern Voting Rights Act

We are now living in the midst of a protracted, concerted, and malevolent assault on voting rights: the Republican Party's long game of using legal machinations to drive down turnout, particularly in heavily Democratic areas, through the imposition of restrictive voter-ID laws that have an obvious and disproportionate impact on communities of color, and the elimination of early voting practices that are disproportionately used by Democratic voters. The Department of Justice under the administration of George W. Bush stood aside while the first wave of such laws was implemented in the early- to mid-2000s. And now the Trump Administration seems intent not just on abetting this effort to steal elections and intentionally depress turnout but also to spark a mass hysteria over false claims that millions of undocumented immigrants voted in the 2016 election. These revanchist and reactionary efforts, plotted and carried out by the inheritors of and spiritual successors to the Jim Crow South, deserve and must receive a much more aggressive response the next time Democrats take power. That response should be a new Voting Rights Act, one that nationalizes federal elections and uses the clear language of the Fifteenth Amendment (which grants Congress the power to prevent voting discrimination based on race, color or "previous condition of servitude") to argue that Congress has the right to guarantee voting rights for all Americans. This legislation must abolish voter-ID laws, create a system of automatic registration, create a national federal holiday for elections, restore the voting rights of all adults in and out of prison, and impose incredibly harsh terms on states that refuse to comply, up to and including unseating congressional delegations from holdout territories. These changes are a moral imperative that might finally fulfill the broken promise of the civil rights era. But it is important to recognize that they are also part of a political battle, that the GOP has for many years systematically used restrictions on voting rights to artificially inflate their electoral gains, and that Democrats must respond in kind if they ever want to fight on a level playing field.

The U.S. Constitution rather infamously neglects to guarantee the right to vote. At the founding, the matter was left to the states, most of whom extended the franchise only to white, male property owners. As Michael Waldman argues, "This refusal to set a national standard, any standard, would have lasting consequences. It left in the hands of state governments one of the most basic elements of national citizenship."[184] The subsequent history of the country is marked by the slow, hard-won expansion of voting rights followed by what Ari Berman has termed "counter-revolutions"[185]—efforts to undo the progress of reformers and return American society to its rightful owners—white men. Time and again, measures that expanded voting rights have provoked a backlash from the forces of white, male supremacy. The Constitution was amended twice in the aftermath of the Civil War in an effort to guarantee voting rights for African American men—only to be, in the end, frustrated by a series of discriminatory laws (preposterously upheld by the reactionary Supreme Court) that deprived African Americans across the U.S. South of the right to vote. Women were granted the franchise only after a decades-long struggle for suffrage via constitutional amendment—the same procedure that was used to lower the voting age from twenty-one to eighteen. Many states, though, still make it as difficult as possible for college students to vote. And the country finally started the process of restoring the franchise to African Americans in the South with the 1965 passage of the Voting Rights Act, just to see modern Republicans implement subtler methods of preventing minorities from casting ballots.

If you aren't familiar with the voting practices of other countries, it may not be immediately obvious how much of a regressive outlier the United States is. There are organizations that focus on electoral and voting systems, like International IDEA (the Institute for Democracy and Electoral Assistance), but they are little known in the United States, where there is a prevailing and at this point wildly unearned sense that America operates the world's most advanced and functional representative democracy. This is a shame, because the democratic world outside of the United States is richly endowed with creative solutions to the quandaries inherent in representative democracy. Huge problems whose existence and persistence we take for granted in the United States—like the fact that barely half of our eligible population deems voting in our elections an act worth participating in, or that we should be forced to conduct them on a regular working Tuesday in late fall, when the weather has already turned punitively miserable in the northern half of the country.

Our generally low turnout rate and the timing of U.S. elections are not intrinsically the result of a desire to exclude voters from the system. But to these happenstance exclusionary practices American democracy has added a series of deliberate provocations, transparently designed mostly by Republicans to prevent poor people and minorities from ever voting at all, or placing enough procedural roadblocks in front of them that they don't bother trying. The statistics around U.S. elections are stark, and as bad as they are in presidential election years, they are worse during midterm elections or, God help you, completely off-year elections when a handful of states hold their gubernatorial and state legislative elections. Just 36.4 percent of the voting-eligible population turned out for the 2014 midterm elections that handed the Senate, and thus ultimately the swing seat on the Supreme Court, to the Republican Party.[186] Globally, these figures are hugely embarrassing. Just 55.7 percent of voting-age Americans voted in the 2016 election, a figure that is more than 30 percent behind turnout in Belgium (87.2%), Sweden (82.6%), Australia (78%), and lags well behind a long list of other countries that includes Greece, Mexico, Iceland, and South Korea.[187]

To address both these embarrassingly low turnout figures, as well as the racist policies put into place by state government after state government this century, Democrats should pass a comprehensive new Voting Rights Act. While some would argue that Congress does not have the authority to mandate changes in state voting practices, this argument does not withstand scrutiny. Indeed, provisions of the original 1965 Voting Rights Act were struck down by the Roberts Court not because Congress lacks the authority to regulate elections, but because it treated some states differently than others. A comprehensive new Modern Voting Rights Act would almost certainly withstand court challenges (with near certainty turning into total certainty if Democrats have the courage to add justices to the Supreme Court), and ideally would include four main pieces: the restoration of voting rights for all felons even when they are still in prison, the creation of a system of automatic voting registration that places the responsibility for registering citizens on the state rather than on overburdened citizens themselves, the declaration of a federal holiday for all federal elections and the abolition of all voter ID laws.

## VOTER SUPPRESSION

In the 2016 election, voter suppression methods are widely and credibly believed to have handed at least Wisconsin to Donald Trump, who carried the state by the agonizing, difficult-to-swallow tally of 27,257 votes. The Badger State, once a stronghold of progressive thinking about government and society, has been ruled since 2010 by a union-busting college dropout called Scott Walker, whose survival of three different elections should probably have been regarded as a warning signal by national Democrats about their fortunes in the state. Like nearly every Republican elected to office since the turn of the century, Walker and his allies in the state legislature made it a priority both to kneecap the state's unions—which are critical GOTV centers for Democrats—and to pass needless legislation addressing the nonexistent problem of voter fraud. Despite promising the state's voters that no one would be disenfranchised by it, the new voter ID law passed in 2011 by a compliant legislature and signed by the unctuous Walker was obviously designed to prevent those living at the margins of society—who are overwhelmingly likely to be Democratic-leaning voters—from casting a ballot at all. The people who wrote the law knew this. The people who signed the law knew this. You would have to bundle yourself up in multiple layers of cashmere denial not to understand that the only purpose of voter ID legislation is to prevent poor people and minorities from showing up at the polls and tossing their Republican overlords into the trash fire. By the time the 2016 election rolled around, 300,000 Wisconsin voters lacked the necessary identification to vote in the presidential election,[188] and if you've got a calculator or you're superquick on the math draw, you can probably see that this number is much larger than the margin by which Trump won the state's ten electoral votes and thus the right to use our tax dollars flying back and forth between Trump branded estates for gullible rich people.

Wisconsin, of course, is not the only swing state to feature one of these Jim Crow Throwback Tuesday laws—in nearly every state where Republicans captured unfettered power between 2010 and 2016, the craven social Darwinists currently in charge of the GOP crafted a series of nearly identical laws. Laws requiring government-issued photo IDs to vote went into practice in Alabama, Mississippi, New Hampshire, South Carolina, Rhode Island, Tennessee, Texas, Virginia, and Wisconsin just since 2010.[189] Other states, like Kansas, passed laws requiring "documentary proof of citizenship" although not necessarily a photo ID. Many such efforts, including those in North Carolina, have been stuffed with other transparently antidemocratic provisions, like cutting back on early voting and trimming the number of voting places. North Carolina's was so egregious that even the Roberts Court struck it down. The number of people disenfranchised by these laws varies by state, but in the aggregate the statistics are jaw-dropping. In 2013, a Texas District Court ruling found that 608,000 duly-registered Texas voters did not have the requisite ID to vote in the state.[190]

The problem allegedly solved by these laws, voter fraud, basically does not exist anymore on a scale large enough to require regressive laws to prevent it. Yes, fraud was once a significant problem in American democracy. But the idea that Chicago chicanery sealed the 1960 presidential election for John F. Kennedy by stuffing the ballots is not very well substantiated by the scholarly evidence.[191] Indeed, a recount was performed, and it did not add nearly enough votes to Richard Nixon's tally in Illinois. This was also fifty-five years ago and counting. Yet many Americans still seem to believe that the old "vote early and often" maxim is something that motivates actual human beings in our society to either cast multiple ballots in the same election or, even more absurdly, to vote in one election in one state and then cross state lines to vote in another one, *on the same day.* I want you to stop for one second and think about how likely it is that more than a tiny handful of people are going to do this. First of all, the penalties for voter fraud are extremely harsh. And the likelihood of any one vote influencing the outcome of an election are minuscule (though not nonexistent). Andrew Gelman, Nate Silver, and Aaron Edlin estimated, based on 2008 election data, that even in the swingiest of swing states like Virginia, Colorado, and New Mexico, that the odds of any one vote influencing the outcome of a presidential election were 1 in 10 million[192]—not good enough for most people to drop $5 on a lottery ticket, let alone risk actual jail time. It is unlikely that you have ever met anyone in your entire life who has intentionally committed voter fraud.

This intuition is borne out by the available evidence, which strongly suggests that the GOP voter fraud panic is entirely fictional and that vote fraud is vanishingly rare. A long list of scholarly articles affirms that impersonation—the only kind of voter fraud protected against by Voter ID laws—is incredibly rare. A 2014 study by law professor Justin Levitt found only thirty-one instances since 2000 of people showing up at the polls pretending to be someone else and casting what is effectively a fake ballot.[193] Another 2014 study confirmed that no significant voter fraud occurred in the 2012 national election, and that states without strict Voter ID laws were no more likely to see cheating than those states that had passed them.[194] These laws incontrovertibly affect minorities, the indigent, and young people more than any other Americans, and therefore they clearly violate the constitutional rights of the voters in these states. Unfortunately, that is not how the United States Supreme Court has seen fit to rule on these matters. In the 2008 case *Crawford v. Marion County Election Board*, SCOTUS ruled that Indiana's voter ID law did not violate the Constitution. Even Justice John Paul Stevens joined the majority in this case, arguing that the law placed only "a light burden on voters."[195] While the Court has refused to hear appeals to lower court decisions on voter-ID laws in North Carolina and Texas, the current body is clearly OK with voter ID laws in theory.

Shortly after he was inaugurated as America's forty-fifth president, Donald Trump issued a long series of dementia-addled Tweets and statements suggesting that illegal immigrants provided the margin of victory for Hillary Clinton in the popular vote. There is, of course, no evidence at all for this either, at least not provided by anyone with a shred of credibility. One reputable 2014 study concluded that "the likely percent of non-citizen voters in recent US elections is 0."[196] Yet the media treated Forty-Five's unhinged and bizarre statements as worthy of further inquiry, invited total hucksters on TV to talk about it, and then Trump's kleptocracy appointed Kansas Secretary of State Kris Kobach, a man who looks a lot like a young Jack Nicholson after several months of going insane at the Overlook Hotel, to form a commission dedicated to investigating the question.

Republicans have used more than just voter ID laws to suppress the vote, developing a shocking array of new tactics to undermine the right to vote in states across the country. One of their favorites is to aggressively reduce the number of polling places in areas where significant numbers of minorities live. Not all long lines at the polls, to be clear, are the result of voter suppression efforts—overly long ballots are also an issue. But in state after state, newly elected Republican legislators and governors have rolled back procedures like early voting hours, early voting stations, Sunday voting, and more. North Carolina slashed early voting in 2013, as did Ohio in 2014, cutting what had become known as "Golden Week," when you could register and vote at the same time.[197] In 2016, Arizona placed new restrictions on the collection of absentee ballots, putting obstacles in front of voters who rely on this kind of voting.[198] In 2011, Florida reduced its early voting period and added limitations on voter registration drives.[199] That same year, Georgia cut its number of early voting days from forty-five to twenty-one, and West Virginia reduced early voting days from seventeen to ten. In 2013, Nebraska cut five days out of its early voting period.[200] Collectively, these measures are known in political science as "convenience voting," which means basically any policy that allows people to vote outside of their precinct on election day. One estimate suggests that convenience voting increases turnout by between 2 percent and 4 percent, depending on the exact basket of procedures put into place.[201] They are believed to boost turnout among groups who lean Democratic more than others. This is why in recent years

Democrats have banked as many early votes as possible, hoping to ride out a loss in election-day voting itself.

As with most of the other worst features of our political system, there is no need for any of this, and other societies have long since discovered useful innovations that not only prevent reactionaries from gaming the system for themselves, but that also encourage the thoughtful participation of all citizens in the electoral system. The Constitution says absolutely nothing about voter registration. It says nothing about the electoral system that we have chosen for ourselves, whose contours lead almost inexorably to the emergence of two large "catch-all" political parties and the near-total exclusion of third parties. This is not an oversight. The Framers of the U.S. Constitution were doing their work in an era in which very little was understood about representative democracy, and indeed the document that they produced at the time contained monumental exclusions—of women, nonproperty owners, and of course, slaves. The men who crafted the Constitution were operating under the belief that democracy, as Sean Wilentz argues, "although an essential feature of any well-ordered government, was also dangerous and ought to be kept strictly within bounds."[202] They had no real model, not just of precisely how to organize and manage the relationships between the different institutional features of their new democracy, but especially of how voting should be conducted for local, state, and national offices.

Elections in the early American republic were conducted so radically differently from today that it is difficult to convey how cracked they would seem to contemporary voters. As recounted entertainingly by the *New Yorker*'s Jill Lepore, "Nowhere in the United States in 1859 did election officials provide ballots." Individuals brought ballots that were preprinted by political parties, or clipped them out of newspapers like a grocery store coupon. As Lepore notes, "Then they had to cross through the throngs to climb a platform placed against the wall of a building (voters weren't allowed inside) and pass their ballots through a window and into the hands of an election judge."[203] Intimidation and fraud were rampant, as was the buying and selling of votes by party bosses and other scoundrels. Violence was not unusual. As Michael Waldman notes of the era, "Evidently a reasonable level of background mayhem was not deemed particularly newsworthy."[204] The idea that the state itself should print ballots, distribute them and supervise the voting process objectively would have struck the Framers as insane, especially since the first elections didn't use paper ballots at all. One can assume that the government also did not require hand-drawn-portrait-IDs to prove that you were a citizen, seeing as how photography itself was not invented until 1826 or so.

But the Constitution's absence of guidance on these issues, ironically, can really tie the hands of originalists who would seek to challenge changes to our laws. Voting is another area where the interests of the contemporary Democratic coalition and the precepts of democratic theory line up neatly. There are those who argue, absurdly, that staying home signals some kind of fundamental satisfaction with our political life (rather than the reality, which is the total alienation from it on the part of millions of hardworking Americans), the truth is that no serious democratic theorist would argue that it is a good thing when people stay home and binge-watch Netflix rather than doing their civic duty. For Democrats, it is clear that the party generally does better when more American voters show up. Just a tiny fraction of Obama voters who stayed home in Michigan, Pennsylvania, and Wisconsin appears to have put Trump narrowly over the top in those states and therefore into the White House. The party has certainly won lower-turnout elections in the past—look no further than Bill Clinton's layup in the 1996 presidential elections—but trends in partisan identification and stratification suggest that the party's fortunes are directly tied to efforts to get people to the polls. Of course, some people will sit out elections no matter what laws and procedures are used. And others could be motivated to participate if Democrats were able to advance a more coherent agenda that clearly links their policies with the fortunes of the downtrodden. But many others could be activated through a series of relatively simple legal changes that could be instituted by simple acts of Congress. The new Voting Rights Act should invalidate all voter-ID statutes and mandate expansive early and absentee voting practices. But it should definitely not stop there.

## AUTOMATIC VOTER REGISTRATION

The United States should also completely overhaul its registration practices to boost turnout and make the franchise available to people who are currently excluded from it. Congress must therefore pass a law demanding that states implement automatic voter registration, creating an "opt out" system for registration rather than an "opt in." The first and most important reason is that registration is much too difficult in far too many places in the United States, creating needless confusion as states use a multiplicity of systems to keep track of voters. Heather Gerken notes that "a recent Pew study reveals that at least 24 percent of the eligible voting population isn't registered. One in eight registrations in the United States is either invalid or contains significant inaccuracies. Nearly two million dead people are on the rolls, 2.75 million people are registered in more than one state, and 12 million voter records contain incorrect addresses."[205] Haphazard data collection and maintenance mean that precious time is wasted by poll workers seeking to confirm the identity of voters.

It is long past time for Congress to fix this situation. No one will be forced to remain registered if they don't want to be. Individuals, if they truly do not want to be registered to vote in the United States, would have to take the step of deregistering themselves and paying the nominal fine for non-voting. Beyond that, Congress could require states to use the data in existing government databases to automatically register citizens to vote. Because the 1993 "Motor Voter Law" that required states to offer voter registration opportunities when citizens applied for or renewed their drivers' licenses easily withstood constitutional challenge, it is unlikely that conservatives could gut automatic voter registration with a well-orchestrated court plan. Therefore, the new Modern Voting Rights Act should require that the United States join so many of its fellow democracies, including France and Sweden, that automatically registers its citizens to vote and consequently enjoy higher levels of voter turnout in national elections. There are a variety of ways to go about this—by using existing records for Social Security, for instance, or census data—but Democrats should also not underestimate the logistical challenge of getting everyone accurately registered, and must have a clear plan for how to implement this law quickly and in time. There is some movement on the automatic voter registration front at the state level—nine states plus D.C. have passed some form of this law.[206] But as Ari Berman notes, "it's also true that too many states are still making it difficult to participate in the political process, by requiring proof of citizenship to register to vote, eliminating same-day voter registration, hindering voter registration drives, and failing to comply with the NVRA."[207] But waiting for each of the fifty states (well, fifty-eight if I have my way), to pass and sign automatic voter registration bills could literally take decades. The better path is for the next Democratic majority to include automatic voter registration in a comprehensive bill and to pass it quickly.

## VOTING FOR EX-FELONS

In a number of U.S. states, anyone convicted of a felony is deprived of the franchise forever. In others, they lose it for a set period of time. The stigma around incarceration means that many people who do serious time in prison never vote again. Particularly because the United States has the highest rate of incarceration of any democratic society in the history of the world, this means that our laws and procedures egregiously drive down turnout across the country and in all elections, in ways that completely contradict the spirit of our criminal justice system, which deems those released from prison to be rehabilitated. Yet many states do not welcome ex-felons back into the fold of democratic society at all. The most egregious are Kentucky, Florida, and Iowa, which permanently strip anyone with a felony conviction of their voting rights for the rest of their lives.[208] Considering the pivotal role that Florida has played in multiple close U.S. elections recently, including in 2000 and 2004, the lack of voting rights for ex-felons—who are disproportionately minorities and who would obviously provide huge margins for the Democrats—the state's laws are both deeply unjust and electorally distorting. To see how reversing these laws might help Democrats, consider the 2017 election in Virginia. Democratic Governor Terry McAuliffe had moved unilaterally to restore the voting rights of 168,000 ex-felons. It might not be a coincidence that Democrat Ralph Northam blew out his polling projections there.

Christopher Uggen and Jeff Manza argue convincingly that Florida's punitive felon disenfranchisement laws altered the outcome of the 2000 presidential election. They write, "If disenfranchised felons in Florida had been permitted to vote, Democrat Gore would certainly have carried the state, and the election."[209] Ari Berman, citing research by the Civil Rights Commission authored by Edward Hailey, suggests that Florida also wrongly disenfranchised 12,000 voters, 44 percent of them African American, by purging them from rolls with faulty matches to the felony database. Had those voters not been falsely excluded from the 2000 election, Berman argues that there would have been 4,752 African-American votes for Al Gore, thus putting him far over the top.[210] Uggen and Manza also found that these disenfrachisement laws flipped seven Senate races from Democrats to Republicans between 1978 and 2000, and since their 2002 article came out, there have likely been many more cases in which a senate seat went to the GOP instead of the Democrats for this reason. Statutes in other states vary widely, but only Maine and Vermont out of all fifty states feature no disenfranchisement for felons at all. In some states, voting rights are restored automatically; in others, like New York, ex-felons must apply to have their rights restored only after their parole is completed. In Arizona, ex-felons may have their voting rights restored after the entire sentence, including prison, parole, and probation, has been served, but anyone with more than one felony conviction is disenfranchised permanently. Other states, like Nevada, permanently disenfranchise people with certain kinds of felony convictions but not others.

Taken together, these restrictions led to 6.1 million Americans being deprived of their voting rights for the 2016 election,[211] a contest that was decided by 70,000 votes spread across Pennsylvania, Michigan, and Wisconsin. It is quite likely that if we had better, more inclusive laws for restoring voting rights for felons, that neither George W. Bush nor Donald Trump would ever have been elected president, and that Democrats would control the U.S. Senate *right now*. For these political reasons, as well as the rank injustice of imposing permanent penalties on citizens who have paid their debt to society, the next unified Democratic government should invalidate all felony voting laws, granting all voting-age Americans the right to vote, even from prison. In fact, the recommendation here is that Democrats should invalidate all felony voting laws, granting all voting-age Americans the right to vote even from prison. While this maximal position has greater political exposure than simply restoring rights for ex-felons, it would again put the United States on more equal footing with fellow democracies like Israel, Canada, the Czech Republic, Austria, and others who impose no voting penalties on criminals whatsoever. This is particularly true given how much of an outlier the United States is in terms of the number of citizens it hits with felony convictions in the first place, which is by far the highest in the developed, democratic world.

## A NATIONAL ELECTION DAY

One of the easiest fixes to our voting system—the low-hanging fruit to end all long-hanging fruits—is to pass a law instituting a national election holiday. The United States is the only country in the advanced democratic world not to do this. Voting is so ingrained in the politically aware public sphere—from pundits to politicians—that few stop to consider how difficult it is for working people to make the sacrifice. Particularly for people toiling in low-wage industries who may not feel safe asking for the day or even an hour off, the lack of accommodation can make the difference between voting and staying home. In the more northerly parts of the country—from snow-menaced rust belt cities like Buffalo to the Great Plains, early November is often nightmarishly cold and accompanied by massive blizzards of the sort that might convince the casual voter that it would be better to hurry home and catch up on *Stranger Things* than to make whatever sacrifices are necessary to get to the polling station. Creating a federal holiday for elections is such a deliriously, unfathomably easy thing to do that it boggles the mind that it has never occurred to lawmakers to craft the legislation to make it so. You could write that law in ten minutes with a handful of second-years from the nearest lawyer factory. Of course, a federal holiday does not relieve many low-income workers in industries like retail and food service from their obligation to work, but a holiday could also put pressure on employers to give their workers the day off, or to carve out some extra space in the day so that they might participate in elections. While one study showed that countries who moved their elections to the weekend did not see an increase in turnout,[212] there is certainly nothing to suggest that a holiday would make things worse. It might take a few cycles for the new reality to set in, but a national election holiday, or weekend voting (or both), could contribute significantly to raising turnout, particularly for those voters who are most disadvantaged by the current system.

In tandem with the national election holiday, Democrats should also address disparities in the availability of polling places. It is not a coincidence that most pictures and stories of achingly long voting lines come from dense urban areas that tend to hold the most Democratic voters—restricting or cutting back on polling places is a time-tested GOP tactic to drive down turnout in urban areas. The Brennan Center estimates that 10 million Americans had to wait half an hour or longer to vote, something that is a huge deterrent to turnout and that causes many people to walk away in frustration. The DNC estimated that 3 percent of Ohio's voters gave up and went home due to long lines during the hotly contested 2004 presidential election. The total number of estimated line-ghosters (174,000) exceeded President Bush's margin of victory (118,000).[213] The New Voting Rights Act should contain language intended to remedy this inequality in voting places and wait times, and must contain provisions to enforce the law against recalcitrant states seeking to use stealth measures to keep white supremacy alive.

The reforms recommended here would best be pursued in tandem rather than piecemeal. By restoring voting rights for ex-felons, eliminating racist voter ID laws, and declaring a national election holiday in a comprehensive new Modern Voting Rights Act, Democrats would instantly add millions of people to the voter rolls in this country, people who would likely vote disproportionately for Democrats. These changes could make the difference in close election after close election, and allow the next Democratic majority to stay in power much longer than it otherwise might.

# Conclusion:

## The Third Reconstruction

It is January 3, 2023. Triumphant Democrats have captured all fourteen Senate seats in the successor states to what was California, as well as all four seats in Puerto Rico and Washington, D.C., to hold a 66 to 50 majority in the chamber. For the first time since 2002, the president's party has gained seats in the midterm elections. In the House, Democrats hold 450 of the chamber's 870 seats, with another 80 for a resurgent Green Party. Together they form a commanding majority bloc over the 280 Republicans and 60 Libertarians. While not without turmoil and some confusion, the new electoral system for the House was carried out without much real controversy.

The 8–5 liberal majority on the Supreme Court is sure to be augmented by the impending retirements of Samuel Alito and Clarence Thomas, who wrote searing dissents in the previous term's landmark cases overturning *Citizens United*, reversing the *Heller* decision, and placing new power in the hands of states and municipalities to restrict gun ownership. After capturing a 55–45 edge in the Senate, a 225–208 House majority and the presidency in 2020, the party finally took the steps to rectify its structural disadvantages in the U.S. electoral system. Democrats then embarked on a furious campaign of progressive legislation: extending health insurance to all Americans through a combination of the public option and lowering the Medicare age to fifty-five, earmarking hundreds of billions for new infrastructure and public transit, creating a Rural Development Authority through the federal government to address the persistent poverty and underdevelopment of so many of the country's forgotten regions, and carving out massive new entitlements to parental leave and low-cost higher education. Freed from the burden of providing healthcare to employees, business is booming, the Dow has reached new heights and the budget is in the black due to the financial transactions law—the so-called Robin Hood tax—passed after the Senate eliminated the legislative filibuster. The 2021 Modern Voting Rights Act reenfranchised millions of Americans, and the 2022 midterms then saw the highest turnout for a nonpresidential election in modern history. This extraordinary blitzkrieg of progressive legislation was made possible because Democrats and their affiliated think tanks meticulously prepared signature-ready legislation prior to the 2020 elections and campaigned on those ideas in all fifty states and in every single congressional district. Analysts credit Democrats and progressives with the "Third Reconstruction"—a crushing victory over the forces of white supremacy, racism, hatred, and selfishness that briefly reigned supreme from 2016 to 2018.[214]

Is this a preposterous scenario? As you are reading this, it probably is. National elections in the United States are simply too monumentally stacked against Democrats for the party to enjoy lasting majorities in Congress and enduring control of the presidency. At best, they can hope to capture power every eight or twelve years, embark on a massive legislative blitz, and hope that their achievements survive the predations of their successors. While the early Trump Administration has failed to roll back all of Obama's achievements, it is a near certainty that they will reverse progress on a number of fronts even if Congressional leaders never recover their ability to marshal legislation through committees and floor votes and to the president's desk for any purpose other than a tax cut for rich people. In the long term, this back-and-forth between a center-left party determined to make serious policy in the public interest, and a gang of antisystem marauders bent on reversing the twentieth century will inevitably lead to worse and worse outcomes for America's poor and middle classes, and invite true planetary disaster.

But aren't all elections simply even playing fields where the team with the best argument wins? Imagine, for a moment, that you went to a baseball game last night (sorry to those of you who think baseball is boring, but you're wrong and I'm right), where you saw your favorite team on the road. Let's say it is the Philadelphia Phillies (OK, OK, I am "you" here) playing in Atlanta against the Braves (ugh, the *Braves.* It is 2018, losers, enough with the racist team names). Your heroes drop a ten-spot in the top of the first inning to take a huge lead, but the Braves score one run an inning for nine straight innings. You go home happy, right? But at the end of the game it's the Braves high-fiving and their fans doing their insane, racist Tomahawk Chop. A hometown fan leans over to you and explains that according to the rules of *this* park, the team that scores in the most number of innings wins, rather than the team that scores the most runs. You just lost a game that you won 10–9. Because those are the rules. The Phillies' players all shuffle off the field shrugging their shoulders like, "What can you do, right?"

For progressives, winning and maintaining power in American politics is just like playing a game of baseball where the rules are rigged to benefit the home team. The problem goes well beyond the electoral college and extends to every crevice of the creaking electoral Victorian that we all inhabit together. Up until now, progressives and Democrats have largely been content to play by a set of rules that is tilted perceptibly against them, mostly because sometimes we win anyway. When the Bush Administration trashed the country in a way that even many Republicans couldn't deny, we won. When President Obama oversaw a gradual recovery from the economic meltdown foisted on the country by the GOP, he won reelection. But too often, Democrats lose when they should win. They have fewer House seats than their percentage of the national vote suggests they should hold. The Senate is a massive structural obstacle to progressive power—not just in the way small states are overrepresented, but also in the way the chamber's rules require supermajorities to do anything. The Supreme Court has had a conservative majority since the 1970s, even though Democrats have won the popular vote in every presidential election since 1992 except 2004. And millions of Democratic-leaning voters are disenfranchised by punitive felony laws and racist voter-ID exclusions, as well as discouraged from voting by America's antiquated registration and election day practices.

The most important thing progressives can do to help transform the United States into a more equal, just, and prosperous society is to win elections—not just in 2018 but in 2020 and beyond. Individuals who care about the future trajectory of this country must get involved, both in local and national politics—join organizations like Indivisible, Democracy For America, and MoveOn, get involved in your local progressive party chapters, get your boots on the ground in the run-up to election days, or if you can't be there or if you're too far from a swing district (check Swing Left to see your closest competitive district), make some phone calls, give until it hurts and make sure that when you wake up the day after the election you feel like you did everything you could, even if it's just a few dollars or hours, to help bring progressive representatives to power. Once they are there, hold them accountable, and tell them that the electoral reforms in this book are important to you. It is no longer enough to win one or two elections in a row and coast on the glow of victory. The left must win multiple state and national elections in a row and then use its newfound power to transform the electoral landscape in ways that will benefit future generations.

That is why progressives must push for, and Democrats must adopt, a series of interrelated political reforms: statehood for Washington, D.C. and Puerto Rico, the breakup of blue behemoth California into seven or more states, the expansion of the House of Representatives, and the replacement of winner-take-all elections with ranked-choice voting, the addition of several liberal jurists to an enlarged Supreme Court while expanding the federal judiciary, and a new Modern Voting Rights Act that includes automatic voter registration, relief from punitive felony voting laws, the elimination of racist ID requirements, and a national election holiday. To be in a position to gain power, Democrats must ruthlessly ape their Republican tormentors by obstructing, delaying, and delegitimizing President Trump and the Republicans until the day they take office. And when they do, they must be willing to discard what remains of, in particular, most Senate traditions like the legislative filibuster. They must act like a duly constituted majority with a mandate to govern and to transform American politics into a fully functional modern social democracy.

The recommendations in this book, if pursued vigorously and defended properly, have the power to transform the American electoral system, from one in which many Americans either choose to stand apart from, or from which they are excluded by law, to one that encourages the participation of an overwhelming majority of the American people. The United States has not made serious changes to its electoral system since the Progressive Era, and the resulting stasis has meant that the United States has fallen seriously behind its peers in the advanced democratic world in terms of how it operates its electoral system. The Republican Party has been the clear beneficiary of exclusionary laws and antiquated electoral practices and stands apart as the only significant political party in the world that seeks to decrease rather than increase the participation of citizens in the electoral process. Cloaked in abject nonsense about voter fraud, GOP leaders have ruthlessly pressed their electoral advantage through voting chicanery, and have availed themselves of seemingly every opportunity to do things like restrict ballot access, decrease opportunities for early and remote voting, and impose new hardships on voters who are also members of the country's most marginalized groups and economic classes. They have been able to do this largely because critics of these practices have never before succeeded in settling on a strategy to fight back, and because Democrats hold total power in so few states that they have been unable to go through with reforms.

But a darker truth lurks behind U.S. lollygagging on modernizing its democracy: we are, all of us, still living with the profound negative consequences of the compromises made at the constitutional convention to placate the beneficiaries of chattel slavery as well as white male property owners of all kinds. As James McPherson argues, "In antebellum America, Southerners controlled the national government most of the time until 1860 and they used that control to defend slavery from all kinds of threats and perceived threats."[215] Nearly all of the postrevolutionary presidents were Southern slaveholders. The states of the American South continued, after the Civil War, to be responsible for so many of America's worst impulses and most reckless decisions, including the project to destroy the future of generations of African Americans by short-circuiting Reconstruction and then consigning Southern blacks to another hundred years of poverty, exclusion, and marginalization. White American men, with their fundamentalist readings of the Constitution as protecting private property above all else, were responsible for stalling important features of the modern welfare state for decades at a clip, and forcing reformers to come up with elaborate workarounds to the obstinacy of the Supreme Court. Why else do you think we needed to pass a constitutional amendment to be able to have an income tax in this country? Why else is the right of corporations to blow unlimited amounts of untraceable cash on the nearest Randian robot running for office now enshrined in constitutional jurisprudence? Why else has the Supreme Court refused to recognize or remedy problems as screamingly obvious as unequal funding for public education, or equal treatment under the law in the criminal justice system? These stubborn ideological blind spots are the inevitable consequence of getting hitched to the U.S. South in a shotgun marriage. There were many other possible futures. This is ours.

Of those compromises made with Southern states, slavery was by far the most destructive, indefensible, inhumane, and cruel. In some important ways, aggressively reforming the electoral system would finally fulfill some of the promises of the early Reconstruction period in American history. Most important, they would eliminate most of the residue of the compromises made at the founding by elites who were forced to bargain with slaveholders in the American South to ensure that the republic could be born and survive. When air-conditioning finally made it bearable for more people to live in the South, a long-term migration from cold-weather areas to the Sun Belt granted a neoconfederacy renewed power over American politics, which apologists for slaveholders and revanchists seeking to preserve white supremacy have used ever since to disadvantage minorities and collect more power than they are due. It is long past time that we break, for good, this Southern stranglehold on American politics.

Breaking up California and granting statehood for Washington, D.C. and Puerto Rico would go a long way toward mitigating the astonishing imbalance of power in the U.S. Senate demanded by small states at the founding. Adding seats to the U.S. House and changing how its members are elected would give greater power and more equal representation to America's urban areas, where so many marginalized minorities are concentrated today, in part to avoid persecution in more far-flung regions where racist reactionaries and their eager executioners hold power. And altering the structure of the Supreme Court and the federal judiciary would give Democrats a once-in-a-generation opportunity to ensure that a full-throated progressive agenda, including the nationalization of the health care system, free public college education for all Americans, and more, could survive the inevitable court challenges that are as certain to be launched within days of any legislation being passed as the sun is to rise in the east tomorrow morning. That progressive future, now there for the taking if Democrats can only seize the opportunity to seize the opportunity, would finally make real the Constitution's lofty language about equality and rights and deliver a crushing blow to the hopes of today's ascendant "alt-right" neo-Nazis who have, shockingly, captured control of the Republican Party. Think of it as a Third Reconstruction, one that will finish the work of the original post–Civil War radical Republicans and LBJ's 1960s civil rights coalition.

To make sure that these changes are as permanent as possible, though, requires that the next Democratic majority break the stalemate in national U.S. politics and avoid the cyclical fate that has awaited both parties since the end of the New Deal era in American life—that at the end of two or three terms dominated by one party, bored and indifferent voters will elect to toss out the incumbents and replace them wholesale with their opponents. This is what happened to the Democrats at the end of the Clinton years, to the Republicans at the end of the Bush era, and then again to the Democrats after eight years of Barack Obama in the White House. If the next generation of victorious Democrats is swept away after four or eight years, it won't matter that they passed Medicare-For-All or raised taxes on the wealthy. Republicans will simply wipe away that progress in a matter of months.

If Democrats can't stay in power for an extended period of time, the dream of conservative judicial radicals stretching back to the Four Horsemen may very well come true—a majority of originalists on the Court will roll back labor protections, oversee the gutting of the social safety net, overturn *Roe v. Wade* and bring back what some like to call The Constitution-in-Exile. This austere, absurd vision offers a bleak future to today's Americans. Adrift in an interconnected world of global capital and trade flows, we will all be completely on our own, vulnerable to total ruin by illness, bankruptcy, or personal misfortune. The yawning inequality that already threatens the democratic experiment will become infinitely worse after a sustained period of Republican rule, as nonelites will have increasing difficulty finding good-paying jobs, affordable housing, accessible education, and high-quality healthcare. In fact, further economic disaster inflicted on the country by self-interested Republican elites will shake the very foundations of representative democracy, as citizens will lose faith in a government that clearly does not care about their welfare and is not interested in pursuing policies that benefit anyone other than their donors, the racist white revanchists at the core of their coalition, and the tiny elite of upper-middle class and uber wealthy beneficiaries of global capital.

Nothing here should be read as suggesting that Democrats should not also come into office with an expansive, aggressive, and radical policy agenda. Fixing our electoral politics and pursuing a string of long-sought progressive dreams are complementary goals rather than mutually exclusive ones. The most important goals of the next Democratic government should be the reduction of inequality, the elimination of discrimination, and the implementation of policies that make it more difficult for ordinary Americans to be ruined by misfortune or bad luck. Importantly, a radical economic agenda is probably the only hope for Democrats to win back the trust of rural voters. To do so they should pursue not only longstanding planks in the party's platform like a higher minimum wage and the elimination of barriers to organized labor, but reach for even more disruptive solutions to the galloping problems of the twenty-first century. They should pass a law containing the so-called Robin Hood Tax, which would levy a tiny tax on certain kinds of financial transactions (both Hillary Clinton and Bernie Sanders supported versions of this tax in the 2016 primaries). This tax alone could raise billions of dollars in revenue for much-needed public investment while doing minimal damage to the functioning of markets. Presuming that the GOP succeeds in crippling the Affordable Care Act beyond repair, Democrats should also push for a single-payer health care system, although the view from here is that the party would be better off implementing the long lost "public option" rather than trying to nationalize the whole system at once. Democrats should also experiment with something called the Universal Basic Income (UBI), a new and radical tool designed to ensure that all Americans, regardless of talent, fortune, race, gender, or class background gets to live a life with a guaranteed minimal amount of dignity.[216]

Private prisons should be abolished, marijuana fully legalized, regulated, and taxed, and the War on Drugs declared the miserable failure that it is and always has been. The most progressive policing programs and policies should be made national policy. To win the favor of disgruntled rural voters, Democrats should also propose a massive program of national investment in poor and remote communities modeled on the Tennessee Valley Authority, and promise to locate enormous new federal green energy projects in the worst-off communities. The party should also create or expand existing systems of public transportation, subsidizing rural and secondary-city airports and building, where feasible, extensions of a new national rail network to connect citizens who live far from their nearest major metropolitan area. And it should go without saying that they should green-light a major expansion and nationalization of high-speed rail in the busiest population corridors, particularly the Richmond-Boston megalopolis. The party must also quickly pass an aggressive law mandating family-leave policies for both men and women, something that should appeal to conservatives because childcare costs are one of the most important factors limiting the desire of many Americans to have children in the first place. The damage done to the climate change movement by the Trump presidency must immediately be reversed by rejoining the Paris climate agreement and doggedly pursuing investment and support for green technologies and making a plan to move away from dirty energy as soon as is humanly possible.

This economic plan must be paired with a blitzkrieg designed to reward the party's most faithful supporters: minorities, women, and other marginalized groups in American society. Democrats should pass a new equal pay law for women and minorities, and reintroduce the Equal Rights Amendment. The Justice Department under the next Democratic president should address, in ways that go beyond what even the Holder DOJ team was willing to do, inequities in America's court and prison system. Congress should pass, and the president should sign, a law mandating equal funding for all public education systems in the United States, and should commit to boosting teacher pay and benefits to attract a new generation of the brightest young Americans to the field. Regulations protecting women, transgender Americans and other minorities, like Title IX regulations in higher education, must be restored.

For undocumented immigrants, Democrats should immediately pursue a massive amnesty for the millions of aspiring Americans currently living on the margins of society. Not only would this rectify the terrible injustice of forcing workers to contribute to American society while excluding them from its most important benefits, it would add millions of Democratic-leaning voters to the rolls in key swing states like Texas, Arizona, and Florida. Republicans have always feared that immigration would change the character of American society. Democrats should reward them with their very worst nightmare. In addition to naturalizing millions of new citizens, Democrats must restore the country's pre-Trump commitment to welcoming new citizens from various parts of the world, and boost the number of refugees that we are willing to absorb, within reason. Importantly, Democrats must make it clear that these proposals do not mean that the party stands for that right-wing straw man of "open borders." On the contrary, the party must articulate how and why the United States must continue to have borders, to ration citizenship, and reassure patriotic Americans—the kind of people who salute the flag unironically—that the left is not interested in turning everyone into a "citizen of the world." What the party must stand for, instead, is the most inclusive and generous possible vision of what it means to be an American that the polity can withstand.

Getting to this hopeful vision means pursuing political reforms that will be regarded in some circles as precipitating a national crisis, nothing more so than the plan advanced here to pack the Supreme Court with liberal jurists and to add more federal judgeships. But the undeniable truth is that we already living through a monumental political crisis. It is partly about President Trump, whose gleeful thrashing of governing norms, civility expectations, and respect for the rule of law are doing incalculable damage to the vulnerable guardrails of democracy. The president, however, is merely a symptom of the long march into the ideological wilderness of the party he captured, which has proven in this new century to be almost utterly devoid of public spirit and respect for democratic traditions and practices. It is the only major political party in the entire democratic world that advocates policies that make it harder for citizens to vote, the only conservative party that marries an aggressive ethnonationalist fervor to a lurid vision of stripping the modern state down to its preindustrial shell. Earlier in this book, I described the modern GOP as an antisystem party. The real danger is that the GOP will succeed in tearing down American democracy and building, in its place, a hybrid regime that looks like a democracy but in fact is nothing more than a vehicle for wealthy, white Americans to enrich themselves at our expense while subjecting the rest of us to a grinding nightmare of insecurity, poverty, climate change, and discrimination.

Under normal circumstances, altering the political system, suddenly and in the myriad ways recommending here, would be a dreadful idea. But normal circumstances assume that a functioning democracy is in place. If citizens are basically satisfied with the political system, then the program recommended here would suggest that one party is seeking to change agreed-upon, fair, and deeply respected rules to benefit a narrow elite. But all is not well with American democracy. It is in mortal peril, and the 2018 and 2020 elections may just afford Democrats and their progressive allies one final chance to prevent our society from careening off the highway and into a gulley. If that sounds apocalyptic, that's because the situation facing this country is indeed an end-of-the-world scenario, a crisis just as grave as that faced by our political elites prior to the Civil War itself.

Democrats absolutely must not proceed with business as usual the next time they arrive victorious in D.C. Big changes—laws that could inaugurate a period of progressive dominance unseen since the New Deal coalition ruled the country—are more important than that next fundraising call or making the rounds on the Sunday talk shows. If they kick this opportunity away, they are going to be looking up, once again, at their Republican overlords in 2024 or 2028. And as bad as these Trump visigoths are, the next group of GOP fanatics to take up residence on the Potomac will almost certainly be much worse. At the least, they will likely have as their standard-bearer someone who knows how a bill becomes law, what health insurance actually is, and who is willing to put in the long hours and clever strategizing needed to realize the right's vision of a racist oligarchy unrestrained by laws, norms, or decency.

There are no final victories in politics—like marriage, it is better thought of as a long conversation. No matter how well Democrats do in four years, and no matter how many of this book's recommendations they put into practice, conservatism will receive no ultimate, End of History shellacking at the polls. Political elites and partisans will always mistake the victories of the moment for broader endorsements of every piece of their ideological agendas. Just as Democrats falsely believed that they had achieved a fundamental realignment of U.S. politics after Barack Obama's victory, so too do Republicans now believe that they have cracked the Democratic coalition and brought into existence a new alignment of the white working class with the party's plutocratic elites and formerly marginal racists and white supremacists.

To prevent that revanchist fantasy from becoming a reality, Democrats and their progressive allies must fight. They must fight dirty. They must seize all the tools granted to them by the Constitution and they must not hold back on using any of them because it will strike some people as uncivil or unsportsmanlike. They must not apologize. If they can muster the will to do the things outlined in this book, we might eventually find ourselves, for the first time in our history, with a true representative democracy in which the voices of all citizens are heard equally and in which all Americans, no matter their racial, gender, economic, or social background, can be assured a minimally decent life. Despite all the horrors of the past two years of American history, despite the neo-Nazi rallies and the midnight ICE raids breaking up families and the cruel attempts to savage the health care system and the unconscionable attacks on Muslim-Americans and the resurgence of misogynist hatred and the collapse of trust in the mass media and the ongoing tragedy of police violence against African Americans and the needless, grinding poverty that so many of our fellow citizens face every day, this is still a dream that I believe in, that I must believe in, and that we must make a reality.

Now give me my Shiraz back. I'm thirsty.

# Acknowledgments

It is standard in this space to say what an enormous undertaking writing a book is. But, real talk: writing this book made me feel like a cat hearing a can of industrial chicken runoff popped by a bleary-eyed human at 6 a.m. If this cloud-stored manuscript disappeared in some massive act of cyber-sabotage, I would gladly start writing it again tomorrow morning. But there were hard times, too: evenings spent nursing a beer with the alcohol content of wine while I brainstormed new ways to insult Donald Trump, and afternoons consumed with researching things I love and am fascinated by. (I don't do mornings). So ok, there really weren't very many hard times. To be honest, the hardest thing about writing this book is that space-time unfolded in a universe in which a dollar-store grifter called Donald Trump is the President of the United States. But I still have gratitude to distribute.

First, this project never would have happened without the help and encouragement of my old college friend, fellow campus newspaper editor, and now managing editor at Melville House, Susan Rella. When I emailed Susan in January 2017 with this zany idea, she not only didn't laugh at me as she probably should have, but agreed to forward my writing to her editor. I am forever indebted to her for supporting this project, advocating for it, and then working with me through the editing and revision of the original manuscript. #DrewUniversityForever. I would also like to thank my amazing editor at Melville House, Taylor Sperry, who took a huge chance on me and pitched the project to the publishers before working closely with me to produce the best possible manuscript. Thanks also to everyone at the Melville House Press team, including the publisher Dennis Johnson, my publicist Alex Primiani, and all of the other dedicated individuals working to keep independent publishing vibrant.

I also owe enormous thanks to *The Week* columnist and my former colleague at the Critical Writing Program at the University of Pennsylvania, Damon Linker, who generously put me in touch with an editor at the magazine in April of 2016. That editor, Ben Frumin, can also drink free beers on me for life for his willingness to publish my pieces and for his superb editing. None of this would have been possible had I not been granted that opportunity. Huge thanks also to Nico Lauricella and Jessica Hullinger for their editing work. I would also like to thank University of Michigan Professor Juan Cole, whose well-trafficked website *Informed Comment* frequently carries my work and who was willing to publish just about anything I wrote about the 2016 election. He is due an enormous debt of gratitude. My wife, partner, and inspiration, Sheerine Alemzadeh, is owed some huge thanks as well. A fabulous writer, accomplished lawyer, and non-profit entrepreneur who dedicates her waking hours to fighting for the rights of sexual assault survivors, she nevertheless took time out of her days to read chapters and offer feedback, and was always willing to serve as a sounding board for some of the more outlandish ideas contained within it. She also encouraged me to pursue the book, even though it would take me away from the study of the Middle East, to which I had heretofore committed my professional life.

I would also like to thank several of my colleagues at Roosevelt University: Mike Maly, Associate Provost for Research, who helped secure a 2017 summer research grant for this project, as well as the Dean of the College of Arts & Sciences, Bonnie Gunzenhauser, and the University Provost, Lois Becker, both of whom generously supported my work last summer. I am indebted to the many people who agreed to be interviewed by me about this book, as well, particularly Michael Brown, David Daley, Ezra Levin, Drew Spencer Penrose, and Gabe Roth.

I would also like to thank my amazing parents, Ralph and Jane Faris, who are literally the two greatest humans you could hope to be blessed with, and who have always supported and enriched my writing, as well as my brother Jason Faris, and my sister-in-law Katie Faris. Finally, I'd like to thank the many friends of mine on social media who have consistently shared my work and argued with me in those spaces, especially Andrew Dufresne, Brianne DeRosa, Joanie Mazelis, Beth Canzanese, Samantha Wittchen, Erin Gautsche, Meredith Heagney, Jeannine Love, Gina Buccola, Celeste Chamberland, Margie Rung, Chelsea Schafer, Bill Herman, Dan Dufresne, Keith Schneider, Gabrielle Gray, Phil Maciak, Katie Faris, Sara Byala and so many others. I couldn't have done any of this without you and your belief in and support for my writing. Finally, incomprehensibly huge thanks are due to David Karpf, Naser Javaid, Christian Pedone, Abby Jones, and David Carpman for reading drafts of this work before publication and offering honest and trenchant criticism. The work is vastly stronger for your input; any mistakes, oversights, or errors of interpretation are mine and mine alone.

# Notes

1 Marcetic, Branko. "Nobody For Bloomberg." *Jacobin*. December 19, 2016. https://www.jacobinmag.com/2016/12/nobody-for-bloomberg.

2 Thrasher, Steven W. "Bernie Sanders could have won. That's the Corbyn lesson for America." *The Guardian*, June 9, 2017. https://www.theguardian.com/commentisfree/2017/jun/09/bernie-sanders-jeremy-corbyn-lesson-for-america.

3 Lilla, Mark. "The End of Identity Liberalism." *The New York Times*, November 18, 2016.

4 Milbank, Dana. "There's No Such Thing as a Trump Democrat." *The Washington Post*, August 4, 2017. https://www.washingtonpost.com/opinions/theres-no-such-thing-as-a-trump-democrat/2017/08/04/0d5d06bc-7920-11e7-8f39-eeb7d3a2d304_story.html?utm_term=.f371530970d9.

5 Aronoff, Kate. "Don't Fly Like a GA-06." *Jacobin*. June 21, 2017. https://www.jacobinmag.com/2017/06/jon-ossoff-georgia-special-election-democratic-part.

6 Galvin, Daniel J. and Thurston, Chloe N. "The Democrats' Misplaced Faith in Policy Feedback." *The Forum*, Vol. 15, No. 2 (2017): 333–343. p. 335.

7 Mettler, Suzanne. *The Submerged State: How Invisible Government Policies Undermine American Democracy*. Chicago, IL: University of Chicago Press, 2011. p. 5.

8 Rosenmann, Alexandra. "Americans Don't Know the Difference

Between Obamacare and ACA." *Salon*. January 19, 2017. http://www.salon.com/2017/01/19/kimmel-on-aca_partner.

9 Dropp, Kyle and Nyhan, Brendan. "One-Third Don't Know Obamacare and Affordable Care Act Are the Same." *New York Times*, February 7, 2017.

10 Galvin and Thurston, p. 338.

11 Dionne, E.J. Jr. *Why the Right Went Wrong: Conservatism From Goldwater to Trump and Beyond*. New York, NY: Simon and Schuster, 2016, p. 369.

12 "The Inaugural Address." Whitehouse.gov. January 20, 2017. https://www.whitehouse.gov/inaugural-address.

13 Mortimer, Caroline. "George Bush thought Donald Trump's inauguration was 'some weird s***'." *The Independent*, March 30, 2017. http://www.independent.co.uk/news/world/americas/us-politics/george-w-bush-donald-trump-inauguration-weird-shit-word-ceremony-us-president-a7657246.html.

14 Davis, Julie Hirschfeld and Rosenberg, Matthew. "With False Claims, Trump Attacks Media on Turnout and Intelligence Rift." *The New York Times*, January 21, 2017.

15 Publius Decius Mus [Anton, Michael]. "The Flight 93 Election." *Claremont Review of Books*. September 5, 2016.

16 McElwee, Sean. "Millennials Are Significantly More Progressive Than Their Parents." *The Washington Post*, March 24, 2016. https://www.washingtonpost.com/news/in-theory/wp/2016/03/24/millennials-are-significantly-more-progressive-than-their-parents/?utm_term=.c44efb954f6a.

17 "Gallup Daily: Trump Job Approval." *Gallup*. Ongoing. President Trump's Gallup approval of 37% on March 18, 2017, less than two months after his inauguration, was worse than any number ever registered by President Obama during his eight years in office. http://www.gallup.com/poll/201617/gallup-daily-trump-job-approval.aspx.

18 Weissmann, Jordan. "Trump's Budget Would Kill a Major Student Loan Forgiveness Program, But Only For New Borrowers." *Slate*. May 23, 2017. http://www.slate.com/blogs/moneybox/2017/05/23/trump's_budget_would_kill_the_public_service_loan_forgiveness_program_for.html.

[19] Bromwich, Jonah Engel. "Lawyers Mobilize at Nation's Airports After Trump's Order." *The New York Times*, January 29, 2017. https://www.nytimes.com/2017/01/29/us/lawyers-trump-muslim-ban-immigration.html.

[20] Dougherty, Michael J. "Why Are We Getting Taller As a Species?" *Scientific American*. Date unknown. https://www.scientificamerican.com/article/why-are-we-getting-taller.

[21] "Originalism: A Primer on Scalia's Constitutional Philosophy." *NPR*. February 14, 2016. http://www.npr.org/2016/02/14/466744465/originalism-a-primer-on-scalias-constitutional-philosophy.

[22] Blake, Aaron. "Neil Gorsuch, Antonin Scalia and Originalism, Explained." *The Washington Post*, February 1, 2017.

[23] Goodheart, Eugene. "The Constitution: Dead or Alive." *Society*, Vol. 50, Issue 6 (December 2013): 535–542.

[24] Teles, S. M. *The Rise of the Conservative Legal Movement: The Battle For Control of the Law*. Princeton, NJ: Princeton University Press, 2009, p. 3.

[25] Ibid., p. 137.

[26] Ibid., p. 137.

[27] Finkelman, Paul. "The Living Constitution and the Second Amendment: Poor History, False Originalism, and a Very Confused Court." *Cardozo Law Review*, Vol. 37, Issue 2 (December 2015): 623–662, p. 641.

[28] Glueck, Katie. "Scalia: The Constitution is "dead." *Politico*. January 29, 2013. http://www.politico.com/story/2013/01/scalia-the-constitution-is-dead-086853.

[29] Dahl, Robert. *How Democratic is the American Constitution?* New Haven, CT: Yale University Press, 2002, p. 15.

[30] Ladewig, Jeffrey W. and Jasinski, Matthew P. "On the Causes and Consequences of and Remedies for Interstate Malapportionment of the U.S. House of Representatives." *Perspectives on Politics*, Vol. 6, No. 1 (March 2008): 89–107.

[31] Dahl, *How Democratic Is the American Constitution?* p. 17.

[32] "Americans' Support For Electoral College Rises Sharply." Gallup. December 2, 2016. http://www.gallup.com/poll/198917/americans-support-electoral-college-rises-sharply.aspx.

[33] "Guns." Gallup. Page visited May 29, 2017. http://www.gallup.com/poll/1645/guns.aspx.

[34] Kodjak, Alison. "Congress Still Limits Health Research on Gun Violence." *NPR's All Things Considered*. December 8, 2015. http://www.npr.org/sections/health-shots/2015/12/08/458952821/congress-still-limits-health-research-on-gun-violence.

[35] Friedmann, Sarah. "How to Fight for the Equal Rights Amendment, Because 2017 Is Our Year." *Bustle*. March 22, 2017. https://www.bustle.com/p/how-to-fight-for-the-equal-rights-amendment-because-2017-is-our-year-46123.

[36] Rayfield, Jillian. "Scalia: 14th Amendment Doesn't Protect Women Against Discrimination." Talking Points Memo, January 4, 2011. http://talkingpointsmemo.com/dc/scalia-14th-amendment-doesn-t-protect-women-against-discrimination.

[37] Glass, Ira, Alex Blumberg, Alexandra Seabrook, and Ben Calhoun. "Take the Money and Run For Office." *This American Life*. NPR.org, March 30, 2012.

[38] Klein, Ezra. "The Most Depressing Graphic For Members of Congress." *Wonkblog. The Washington Post*, January 14, 2013. https://www.washingtonpost.com/news/wonk/wp/2013/01/14/the-most-depressing-graphic-for-members-of-congress/?utm_term=.b44e91e4774d.

[39] O'Donnell, Norah. "Are Members of Congress Becoming Telemarketers?" CBS News. April 24, 2016. https://www.cbsnews.com/news/60-minutes-are-members-of-congress-becoming-telemarketers.

[40] Epps, Garrett. "What Does the Constitution Actually Say About Voting Rights?" *The Atlantic*. August 19, 2013. https://www.theatlantic.com/national/archive/2013/08/what-does-the-constitution-actually-say-about-voting-rights/278782.

[41] Linz, Juan J. "The Perils of Presidentialism." *Journal of Democracy*, Vol. 1, No. 1 (Winter 1990): 51–69. p. 52.

[42] The Civil War cannot be blamed on a dispute between the different branches of the federal government.

[43] Linz, Juan J. "The Virtues of Parliamentarism." *Journal of Democracy*, Vol. 1, No. 4 (Fall 1990): 84–91. p. 89.

44 Mayhew, David R. "Is Congress the Broken Branch?" *Boston University Law Review*, Vol. 89, No. 2 (2009): 357–369, p. 362.

45 Mayhew, David R. *Divided We Govern: Party Control, Lawmaking, and Investigations, 1946–2002.* New Haven, CT: Yale University Press, 2005, p. 4.

46 Legislative data is courtesy of GovTrack.

47 "We're Surprisingly Close To Our First Constitutional Convention Since 1787. Bad Idea." *The Washington Post* editorial board. April 6, 2017. https://www.washingtonpost.com/opinions/were-surprisingly-close-to-a-new-constitutional-convention-bad-idea/2017/04/06/f6d5b76a-197d-11e7-855e-4824bbb5d748_story.html?utm_term=.3544c5948c61.

48 Tumulty, Karen and Philip Rucker. "Shouting match erupts between Clinton and Trump aides." *The Washington Post*, December 1, 2016. https://www.washingtonpost.com/politics/shouting-match-erupts-between-clinton-and-trump-aides/2016/12/01/7ac4398e-b7ea-11e6-b8df-600bd9d38a02_story.html?utm_term=.b2d148261610.

49 Karpf, David. "Trump's victory: the morning after." *Shouting Loudly*, November 9, 2016. http://www.shoutingloudly.com/2016/11/09trumps=victory=the=morning=after/.

50 Tushnet, Mark. "Constitutional Hardball." *The John Marshall Law Review*, vol. 37, No. 2 (2004): 523–553, p. 523.

51 O'Neill, Tip, with William Novak. *Man of the House: The Life and Political Memoirs of Speaker Tip O'Neill.* New York, NY: St. Martin's Press, 1987. p. xvi.

52 U.S. Senator Mitch McConnell (R-KY). Victory Speech. November 4, 2014. https://www.youtube.com/watch?v=OYxJjCbXSgY.

53 Mann, Thomas and Norman Ornstein. *It's Even Worse Than It Looks: How the American Constitutional System Collided With the New Politics of Extremism*. New York, NY: Basic Books, 2012.

54 Capra, Frank, dir. *Mr. Smith Goes To Washington.* 1939; Culver City, CA: Columbia Pictures 1939. Amazon Video.

55 Hickey, Walter. "The longest filibuster in history lasted more than a day—here's how it went down." *Business Insider*, March 6, 2013.

http://www.businessinsider.com/longest-filibuster-in-history-strom-thurmond-rand-paul-2013-3.

[56] Mayhew, David R. *Parties & Policies: How the American Government Works*. New Haven, CT: Yale University Press, 2008. p. 274.

[57] Howard, Nicholas O. and Jason M. Roberts. "The Politics of Obstruction: Republican Holds in the U.S. Senate." *Legislative Studies Quarterly*, Vol. 40, No. 2 (May 2015): 273–294. pp. 275.

[58] Oleszek, Mark J. "'Holds' in the Senate." Congressional Research Service. R43563. January 24, 2017.

[59] Yglesias, Matthew. "American Democracy is Doomed." *Vox*. October 8, 2015. https://www.vox.com/2015/3/2/8120063/american-democrcy-doomed

[60] Matthews, Dylan. "This is How the American System of Government Will Die." *Vox*. March 3, 2015. https://www.vox.com/2015/3/3/8120965/american-government- problems

[61] Mickey, Robert, Steven Levistky, and Lucan Ahmad Way. "Is America Still Safe For Democracy?" *Foreign Affairs*, January 2017. https://www.foreignaffairs.com/articles/united-states/2017-04-17/america-still-safe-democracy.

[62] Hetherington, Marc J. and Jonathan D. Weiler. *Authoritarianism & Polarization in American Politics*. Cambridge, U.K.: Cambridge University Press, 2009. p. 191.

[63] "Political Polarization in the American Public." Pew Research Center. June 12, 2014. http://www.people-press.org/2014/06/12/political-polarization-in-the-american-public/?beta=true&utm_expid=53098246-2.Lly4CFSVQG2lphsg-KopIg.1&utm_referrer=https%3A%2F%2Fwww.google.com%2F.

[64] Enochs, Kevin. "In US, 'Interpolitical Marriage' Increasingly Frowned Upon." *VOA News*, February 3, 2017. https://www.voanews.com/a/mixed-political-marriages-an-issue-on-rise/3705468.html.

[65] "Putin's Image Rises in the U.S., Mostly Among Republicans." Gallup, February 21, 2017. http://www.gallup.com/poll/204191/putin-image-rises-mostly-among-republicans.aspx.

[66] "Trump Holds Steady After Charlottesville." Public Policy Polling, August 23, 2017. http://www.publicpolicypolling.com/pdf/2017/PPP

Release_National_82317.pdf. Despite its generally strong reputation among poll-watchers, PPP does have a tendency to ask these kinds of controversial, out-of-left-field questions. For instance, they once asked respondents whether they believed Ted Cruz was the Zodiac Killer.

67 Trende, Sean. "What Has Made Congress More Polarized?" *RealClear-Politics*, May 11, 2012. https://www.realclearpolitics.com/articles/2012/05/11/what_has_made_congress_more_polarized.html.

68 Data can be viewed and sorted at Voteview.com.

69 Mann, Thomas E. and Norman J. Ornstein. *It's Even Worse Than It Looks: How the American Constitutional System Collided With the New Politics of Extremism*. New York, NY: Basic Books, 2012. p. 33.

70 Sartori, Giovanni. *Parties and Party Systems: A Framework For Analysis*. Cambridge, U.K.: Cambridge University Press, 1976. p. 133.

71 Ibid., 133.

72 Flinders, Matthew. *Defending Politics: Why Democracy Matters in the 21st Century*. Oxford, U.K.: Oxford University Press, 2012. p. 39.

73 Sartori, p. 140.

74 Of course, Republicans do not have a monopoly on this kind of behavior—Massachusetts changed the rules for how a Senate vacancy is filled, once in 2004 to *prevent* Mitt Romney from filling John Kerry's seat and then again in 2010 to *allow* Deval Patrick to replace the late Ted Kennedy. One is also reminded of the maneuvering New Jersey Democrats did to replace Roberto Torricelli on the 2002 Senate ballot when he became embroiled in a campaign finance scandal. Nothing in this book should be interpreted to suggest that Democrats have been beyond reproach.

75 Grossman, Matt and David A. Hopkins. *Asymmetric Politics: Ideological Republicans and Group Interest Democrats*. Oxford, UK: Oxford University Press, 2016. p. 11.

76 After Clinton signed the welfare reform bill, he had a 58–35 approval rating on "welfare." See "Clinton Approval Rating," CNN. August 25, 1996. http://www.cnn.com/ALLPOLITICS/1996/polls/cnn.usa.gallup/082596.shtml.

77 Stockman, Farah. "On Crime Bill and the Clintons, Young Blacks

Clash With Parents." *New York Times*, April 18, 2016. https://www.nytimes.com/2016/04/18/us/politics/hillary-bill-clinton-crime-bill.html?mcubz=.

78 "Does It Matter That Senate Republicans Wrote Their Health Care Bill in Secret?" A FiveThirtyEight Chat. June 21, 2017. https://fivethirtyeight.com/features/does-it-matter-that-senate-republicans-wrote-their-health-care-bill-in-secret.

79 "U.S. Voters Oppose GOP Health Plan 3-1, Quinnipiac University National Poll Finds; Big Opposition To Cuts To Medicaid, Planned Parenthood." Quinnipiac University poll, March 23, 2017.

80 Enten, Harry. "Disliking Congress as a whole, and as individuals." *FiveThirtyEight*. July 1, 2014. https://fivethirtyeight.com/datalab/disliking-congress-as-a-whole-and-as-individuals.

81 Mayhew, David R. *Congress: The Electoral Connection*. Hartford, CT: Yale University Press, 1974.

82 Jacobson, Gary C. "It's Nothing Personal: The Decline of the Incumbency Advantage in US House Elections." *The Journal of Politics*, Vol. 77, No. 3 (2015): 861–873, p. 862.

83 Wang, Sam. "What Would it Take for the House to Flip?" Princeton Election Consortium, August 12, 2016. http://election.princeton.edu/2016/08/12/what-would-it-take-for-the-house-to-flip.

84 Kondik, Kyle. "Handful of House Races Move Toward Democrats." *Larry Sabato's Crystal Ball*. August 11, 2016. http://www.centerforpolitics.org/crystalball/articles/house-update-handful-of-races-move-toward-democrats.

85 "Indivisible: A Practical Guide for Resisting Trump's Agenda." http://www.indivisible.org/guide. Washington, DC: 2016.

86 Author interview with Ezra Levin, cofounder of Indivisible, August 18, 2017.

87 Hulse, Carl. "Democrats Perfect Art of Delay While Republicans Fume Over Trump Nominees." *The New York Times*, July 17, 2017. https://www.nytimes.com/2017/07/17/us/politics/senate-democrats-art-of-delay-trump-nominees.html?mcubz=0.

88 Author interview with Ezra Levin, August 18, 2017.

89 Author interview with Ezra Levin, August 18, 2017.

90 Dionne, E.J., Jr., Norman Ornstein, and Thomas Mann. *One Nation After Trump: A Guide For the Perplexed, the Disillusioned, the Desperate and the Not-Yet-Deported.* New York, NY: St. Martin's Press, 2017.

91 Lewis, Tom. *Washington: A History of Our National City.* New York, NY: Basic Books, 2015, p. xxvii.

92 "The D.C. Statehood Vote." Opinion Editorial, *The Washington Post*, November 20, 1993. Page A22.

93 Henderson, Nell. "The Naysayers; Perhaps the most common concern is the economic viability of the new state." *The Washington Post Magazine*, July 4, 1993. Page W25.

94 Ibid.

95 Congressional Record, House. November 21, 1993. Page 18.

96 "H.R. 51—D.C. Statehood Bill. Voting Record. Votesmart.org.

97 Congressional Record, House. November 21, 1993. p. 31514.

98 Author interview with U.S. Senator Michael Brown, June 21, 2017.

99 Whitehead, John S. *Completing the Union: Alaska, Hawai'i and the Battle For Statehood.* Albuquerque, NM: University of New Mexico Press, 2004, pp. 254–255.

100 Pilon, Roger. "D.C. Statehood Is a Fool's Errand." *The National Interest*, June 5, 2016. https://www.cato.org/publications/commentary/dc-statehood-fools-errand.

101 Rozsa, Matthew. "Majority of Americans Don't Realize Puerto Rico is Part of America." *Salon*. September 22, 2017. https://www.salon.com/2017/09/22/majority-of-americans-dont-realize-puerto-rico-is-part-of-america.

102 Barreto, Amílcar Antonio. "American Identity, Congress, and the Puerto Rico Statehood Debate." *Studies in Ethnicity and Nationalism*: Vol. 16, No. 1 (2016): 100–116, p. 106.

103 Duany, Jorge. *Puerto Rico: What Everyone Needs to Know.* Oxford, U.K.: Oxford University Press, 2017. loc. 863.

104 Ibid., loc. 877.

105 Denis, Nelson A. *War Against All Puerto Ricans: Revolution and Terror in America's Colony.* New York, NY: Nation Books, 2015, p. 15.

106 Duany, loc. 911.

107 Denis, p. 139.

108 Duany, loc. 1029.

109 Ford, Gerald R.: "Statement on Proposed Statehood for Puerto Rico," December 31, 1976. Online by Gerhard Peters and John T. Woolley, *The American Presidency Project.* http://www.presidency.ucsb.edu/ws/?pid=5538.

110 Muntaner, Frances Negrón. "Who Decides?: The Puerto Rico Status Melodrama." *Enclave.* June 19, 2017. http://www.enclavemag.com/puerto-rico-status-melodrama.

111 Surowiecki, James. "The Puerto Rican Problem." *The New Yorker.* April 6, 2015.

112 Martinez, Gibrán Cruz. "The end of colonialism in Puerto Rico? Evaluating the options in the 2017 political status referendum." London School of Economics, United States Politics and Policy blog. May 19, 2017.

113 Full disclosure: the first class I ever took in graduate school was taught by Rubinstein. It was on the Middle East. The textbook was *The Godfather.* Swear to God.

114 Rubinstein, Alvin Z. "The Case Against Puerto Rico Statehood." *Orbis*, Vol. 45, Issue 3 (Summer 2001): 415–432, p. 426.

115 Morín, José Luis. "Indigenous Hawaiians Under Statehood: Lessons For Puerto Rico." *Centro*, Vol. XI, No. 2 (2000): 4–25.

116 Haddock, Vicki. "Splitsville: Californians Have Tried—And Failed—200 Times to Divide the State." *California Magazine*, Summer 2012. http://alumni.berkeley.edu/california-magazine/summer-2012-north-south/splitsville-californians-have-tried-and-failed-200-times.

117 Starr, Kevin. *California: A History.* New York, NY: Modern Library, 2005. pp. 105–106.

118 Laufer, Peter. "State of Jefferson." *1859: Oregon's Magazine.* May 1, 2014. https://1859oregonmagazine.com/think-oregon/art-culture/state-of-jefferson.

119 Goodyear, Sarah. "Rebellion in California." *New York Daily News*, February 9, 2016.

120 "Six Californias Initiative (2016). Ballotpedia. https://ballotpedia.org/%22Six_Californias%22_Initiative_(2016).

121 270toWin.com http://www.270towin.com/states/California.

122 Data from the Orange County Registrar of Voters. Elections Archives, available at https://www.ocvote.com/data/election-results-archive/

123 Silver, Nate. "The Five States of Texas." *D Magazine*, July 2009. https://www.dmagazine.com/publications/d-magazine/2009/july/the-five-states-of-texas.

124 Miller, Jim. "Three Californias? Calexit effort joined by new state-splitting plan." *Sacramento Bee*. August 18, 2017. http://www.sacbee.com/news/politics-government/capitol-alert/article168118272.html.

125 Eilperin, Juliet and DeBonis, Mike. "President Obama Nominates Merrick Garland to the Supreme Court." *The Washington Post*, March 16, 2016.

126 RealClearPolitics. "General Election: Trump Vs. Clinton." https://www.realclearpolitics.com/epolls/2016/president/us/general_election_trump_vs_clinton-5491.html.

127 "Supreme Court." Gallup Historical Trends. http://news.gallup.com/poll/4732/supreme-court.aspx

128 See Michelle Malkin's *In Defense of Internment: The Case For Racial Profiling in WWII and the War on Terror*. Washington, D.C.: Regnery Publishing, 2004.

129 Solomon, Burt. *FDR V. The Constitution: The Court-Packing Fight and the Triumph of Democracy*. New York, NY: Walker and Co., 2009, p. 31.

130 Burns, James MacGregor. *Packing the Court: The Rise of Judicial Power and the Coming Crisis of the Supreme Court*. New York, NY: Penguin Books, 2009, p. 251.

131 Ibid., p. 94.

132 "Calculators: Life Expectancy. Social Security Administration." https://www.ssa.gov/planners/lifeexpectancy.html.

133 Toobin, Jeffrey. *The Nine: Inside the Secret World of the Supreme Court*. New York, NY: Anchor Books, 2008. loc. 2115.

134 Calabresi, Steven G. and James Lindgren. "Term Limits For the Supreme Court: Life Tenure Reconsidered." *Harvard Journal of Law & Public Policy*, Volume 29, Issue 3 (Summer 2006): 769–877.

135 Crowe, Justin and Christopher F. Karpowitz. "Where Have You

Gone, Sherman Minton? The Decline of the Short-Term Supreme Court Justice." *Perspectives on Politics*, Vol. 5, No. 3 (September 2007): 425–445. p. 427.

136 "Term Limits." Fix the Court. https://fixthecourt.com/fix/term-limits.

137 You can read the full proposal here. https://fixthecourt.com/2017/06/tlproposal.

138 Author interview with Gabe Roth, Chicago, Illinois, July 3, 2017.

139 Author interview with Gabe Roth.

140 Baker, Thomas E. "On Redrawing Circuit Boundaries: Why the Proposal to Divide the United States Court of Appeals for the Ninth Circuit is Not Such a Good Idea." *Arizona State Law Journal* (1990): 917–961.

141 Bannon, Alicia. "The Impact of Judicial Vacancies on Federal Trial Courts." Brennan Center For Justice, 2014. http://www.brennancenter.org/sites/default/files/publications/Impact%20of%20Judicial%20Vacancies%20072114.pdf.

142 Bendery, Jennifer. "Federal Judges Are Burned Out, Overworked, and Wondering Where Congress Is." *The Huffington Post*. September 30, 2015. https://www.huffingtonpost.com/entry/judge-federal-courts-vacancies_us_55d77721e4b0a40aa3aaf14b.

143 "ABA National Lawyer Population Survey: Historical Trend in Total National Lawyer Population, 1878–2017." https://www.americanbar.org/content/dam/aba/administrative/market_research/Total%20National%20Lawyer%20Population%201878-2017.authcheckdam.pdf.

144 Calabresi, Steven G., and Shams Hirji. "Proposed Judgeship Bill." Northwestern University Pritzker School of Law Public and Legal Theory Series, No. 17-24.

145 Exit polls for the national presidential vote can be found on CNN.com at http://www.cnn.com/election/results/exit-polls.

146 Cushman, Barry. "Court-Packing and Compromise." *Constitutional Commentary*, Vol. 29, No. 1 (2013): 1–30. p. 1.

147 Kyvig, David E. "The Road Not Taken: FDR, the Supreme Court and Constitutional Amendment." *Political Science Quarterly*, Vol. 104, No. 3 (1989): 463–481. p. 481.

148 Weigel, Dave. "Cruz says there's precedent for keeping ninth

Supreme Court seat empty." *The Washington Post*, October 26, 2016.

149 Totenberg, Nina. "If Clinton Wins, Republicans Suggest Shrinking the Size of the Supreme Court." NPR, November 3, 2016. https://www.npr.org/2016/11/03/500560120/senate-republicans-could-block-potential-clinton-supreme-court-nominees.

150 Hammer, Josh. "It's Time For Congress to Declare War on the Judiciary." *The Resurgent*, June 29, 2016. https://www.themaven.net/theresurgent/contributors/it-s-time-for-congress-to-declare-war-on-the-judiciary-QeK4JAnjxEaPyz6yD-RGxQ.

151 Velasco, Julian. "Congressional Control Over Federal Court Jurisdiction: A Defense of the Traditional View." *Catholic University Law Review*, Vol. 46, No. 3 (1997): 671–765, p. 765.

152 Paulsen, Michael Stokes. "The Case for Shrinking the Supreme Court." *National Review*, October 19, 2016. http://www.nationalreview.com/article/441188/supreme-court-2016-election-fewer-justices-would-curb-its-power.

153 Post, Robert C. and Reva B. Siegel. "Originalism as a Political Practice: The Right's Living Constitution." *Fordham Law Review*, Vol. 75, no. 2 (2006): 545–574, p. 549.

154 Burns, James MacGregor. *Packing the Court*, pp. 30–31.

155 Graglia, Lino A. "Rethinking Judicial Supremacy." *Constitutional Commentary*, Vol. 31 (September 2016): 381–387, p. 386.

156 Political scientists object to the term "first past the post" because in U.S. elections there is no "post" to get past. The person with the most votes wins, even if that is less than a majority. Theoretically, if ten candidates ran in most House elections and split the vote almost evenly, a candidate with 11 percent of the vote could win and be sent to D.C.

157 One study showed that presidents and vice-presidents live, on average, 5.3 fewer years than the people they defeated for the office. See Bruce G. Link, Richard M. Carpiano, and Margaret M. Weden. "Can Honorific Awards Give Us Clues about the Connection between Socioeconomic Status and Mortality?" *American Sociological Review*, Vol. 72, No. 2 (2013): 192–212.

158 Author interview with Drew Spencer Penrose, June 18, 2017.

159 I owe this insight to David Daley.

160 Michael J. Barber and Nolan McCarty in Nathan Persily, ed. *Solutions to Political Polarization in America* (Cambridge University Press, 2015) note that "the evidence in support of gerrymandering as a cause of polarization is not strong" and argue that common remedies, such as nonpartisan redistricting, and eliminating partisan primaries, are unlikely to solve the problem, p. 28.

161 Daley, David. *Ratf**ked: The True Story Behind the Secret Plan to Steal America's Democracy*. New York, NY: Liveright, 2016, loc. 172 of 4834.

162 Daley, *Ratf**ked*, loc. 185 of 4834.

163 Author interview with David Daley, June 17, 2017.

164 Ibid.

165 Bishop, Bill. *The Big Sort: Why the Clustering of Like-Minded America is Tearing Us Apart*. New York, NY: Houghton Mifflin, 2008, loc. 637 (Kindle edition).

166 Gamio, Lazaro. "Urban and rural America are becoming increasingly polarized." *The Washington Post*, November 17, 2016. https://www.washingtonpost.com/graphics/politics/2016-election/urban-rural-vote-swing.

167 Linker, Damon. "It's not elites vs. populists: it's cities vs. the countryside." *The Week*, April 18, 2017. http://theweek.com/articles/692620/not-elites-vs-populists-cities-vs-countryside.

168 Daley, *Ratf**ked*, loc. 274 of 4834.

169 "It's Not Just Gerrymandering." FairVote.org. December 16, 2012. http://www.fairvote.org/it-s-not-just-gerrymandering-fixing-house-elections-demands-end-of-winner-take-all-rules.

170 Duverger, Maurice. *Political Parties: Their Organization and Activity in the Modern State*. London: Methuen (1964).

171 Scarrow, Susan. "Political Parties and Party Systems." In Lawrence LeDuc, Richard G. Niemi, and Pippa Norris, eds., *Comparing Democracies: Elections and Voting in the 21st Century*, pp. 50–51. Duverger's Law is often misrepresented as arguing that SMDP leads inexorably to two-party systems. However, it is better thought of as

increasing the probability that a country, province, or city will end up with two major parties, rather than as an iron law.

172 "American's Desire For Third Party Persists This Election Year." Gallup, September 30, 2016. http://news.gallup.com/poll/195920/americans-desire-third-party-persists-election-year.aspx.

173 "American's Desire For Third Party Persists This Election Year." Gallup, September 30, 2016. http://news.gallup.com/poll/195920/americans-desire-third-party-persists-election-year.aspx.

174 Author interview with Drew Spencer Penrose, June 18, 2017.

175 Farrell, David M. and Richard S. Katz. "Assessing the Proportionality of the Single Transferable Vote." *Representation*, Vol. 50, Issue 1 (2014): 13–26, p. 14.

176 Horowitz, Donald L. "Electoral Systems: A Primer For Decision Makers." *Journal of Democracy*, Vol. 14, No. 4 (October 2003): 115–127, p. 124.

177 Farrell, David M., Jane Suiter, and Clodagh Harris. "The challenge of reforming a 'voter-friendly' electoral system: the debates over Ireland's single transferable vote." *Irish Political Studies*, Vol. 32, No. 2 (2017): 293–310, p. 296.

178 Farrell, Suiter, and Harris, p. 298.

179 Ibid., p. 299.

180 "A Representative Congress: Enhancing African American Voting Rights in the South with Choice Voting." Fair Vote. November 27, 2012. http://www.fairvote.org/a-representative-congress-enhancing-african-american-voting-rights-in-the-south-with-choice-voting/.

181 Sadonis, Tyler, and Joe Witte. "The Supply Side: Alternative Reform Approaches to Campaign Finance." Fair Vote. January 26, 2012. http://www.fairvote.org/citizens-united-rebuttal.

182 Phillips, Amber. "House Democrats Are Running Out of Future Leaders." *The Washington Post*, January 6, 2016. https://www.washingtonpost.com/news/the-fix/wp/2016/01/06/house-democrats-are-running-out-of-future-leaders/?utm_term=.3a3ed528b5b9.

183 Ahmed, Amel. *Democracy and the Politics of Electoral System Choice*. Cambridge, U.K.: Cambridge University Press, 2012, p. 7.

184 Waldman, Michael. *The Fight to Vote*. New York, NY: Simon and Schuster, 2016, p. 25.

185 Berman, Ari. *Give Us the Ballot: The Modern Struggle For Voting Rights in America, 2016.*

186 Montanaro, Domenico, Rachel Wellford, and Simone Pathe. "2014 midterm election turnout lowest in 70 years." PBS.org. November 10, 2014. http://www.pbs.org/newshour/updates/2014-midterm-election-turnout-lowest-in-70-years.

187 Desilver, Drew. "U.S. trails most developed countries in voter turnout." Pew Research Center. May 15, 2017.

188 Cassidy, Christina A., and Ivan Moreno. "In Wisconsin, ID law proved insurmountable for many voters." Associated Press, May 14, 2017. https://apnews.com/dafac088c90242ef8b282fbebddf5b56.

189 "Voting Restrictions in Place for 2016 Presidential Election." Brennan Center For Justice. August 2, 2016. https://www.brennancenter.org/sites/default/files/analysis/Restrictive_Appendix_Post-2010.pdf.

190 Roth, Zachary. *The Great Suppression: Voting Rights, Corporate Cash and the Conservative Assault on Democracy.* New York, NY: Crown Books, 2016, p. 39.

191 Kallina, Edmund F. "Was the 1960 Presidential Election Stolen? The Case of Illinois." *Presidential Studies Quarterly*, Vol. 15, No. 1 (1985): 113–118; see also David Greenberg, "Was Nixon Robbed?" *Slate*. October 16, 2000. http://www.slate.com/articles/news_and_politics/history_lesson/2000/10/was_nixon_robbed.html.

192 Gelman, Andrew, Nate Silver, and Aaron Edlin. "What is the Probability Your Vote Will Make a Difference?" *Economic Inquiry*, Vol. 50, No. 2 (2012): 321–326, p. 323.

193 Levitt, Justin. "A comprehensive investigation of voter impersonation finds 31 credible incidents out of one billion ballots cast." *The Washington Post*, August 6, 2014. https://www.washingtonpost.com/news/wonk/wp/2014/08/06/a-comprehensive-investigation-of-voter-impersonation-finds-31-credible-incidents-out-of-one-billion-ballots-cast/?utm_term=.0860b4fed6b5.

194 Ahlquist John S., Mayer, Kenneth R., and Jackman, Simon. "Alien Abduction and Voter Impersonation in the 2012 U.S. General Elec-

tion: Evidence from a Survey List Experiment." *Election Law Journal: Rules, Politics, and Policy*. Vol. 13, No. 4, (460–475).

195 Williams, David. "The Supreme Court and Indiana's Voter ID Law." *Indiana Magazine of History*, Vol. 104 (December 2008): 379–385, p. 382.

196 Ansolabehere, Stephen, Samantha Luks, and Brian F. Schaffner. "The Perils of Cherry Picking Low Frequency Events in Large Sample Surveys." *Cooperative Congressional Election Study*. November 5, 2014. As cited in "Debunking the Voter Fraud Myth." Brennan Center For Justice. January 31, 2017.

197 Rice-Johnson, Phoenix. "A Step in the Wrong Direction: Cutting Early Voting Hurts Voters." Brennan Center For Justice, November 5, 2016. https://www.brennancenter.org/blog/step-wrong-direction-cutting-early-voting-hurts-voters.

198 "Voting Restrictions in Place for 2016 Presidential Election." Brennan Center For Justice.

199 Ibid.

200 Ibid.

201 Gronke, Paul, Eva Galanes-Rosenbaum, Peter A. Miller, and Daniel Toffey. "Convenience Voting." *Annual Review of Political Science*, Vol. 11 (2008): 437–455, p. 442.

202 Wilentz, Sean. *The Rise of American Democracy: Jefferson to Lincoln*. New York, NY: W.W. Norton and Co., 2005, p. 7.

203 Lepore, Jill. "How We Used to Vote." *The New Yorker*. October 13, 2008.

204 Waldman, Michael. *The Fight To Vote*, p. 53.

205 Gerken, Heather. "Make It Easy: The Case for Automatic Registration." *Democracy: A Journal of Ideas*. Spring 2013. http://democracyjournal.org/magazine/28/make-it-easy-the-case-for-automatic-registration.

206 "Automatic Voter Registration." Brennan Center for Justice. July 20, 2017. https://www.brennancenter.org/analysis/automatic-voter-registration. Last updated December 4, 2017.

207 Berman, Ari. "How Automatic Voter Registration Can Transform American Politics." *The Nation*, September 22, 2015. http://www.thenation.com/article/how-automatic-voter-registration-can-transform-american-politics.

208 "Criminal Disenfranchisement Laws Across the United States." Brennan Center For Justice at the New York University School of Law. Last updated October 6, 2016. http://www.brennancenter.org/criminal-disenfranchisement-laws-across-united-states.

209 Uggen, Christopher, and Jeff Manza. "Democratic Contraction? Political Consequences of Felon Disenfranchisement in the United States." *American Sociological Review*, Vol. 67, No. 6 (December 2002): 777–803, p. 792.

210 Berman, Ari. *Give Us the Ballot:* p. 213.

211 Uggen, Christopher, Larson, Ryan, and Shannon, Sarah. "6 Million Lost Voters: State-Level Estimates of Felony Disenfranchisement, 2016." The Sentencing Project. October 6, 2016.

212 Franklin, Mark N. *Voter Turnout and the Dynamics of Electoral Competition in Established Democracies Since 1945*. Cambridge, UK: Cambridge University Press, 2004. p. 15.

213 Berman, Ari. *Give Us The Ballot*. p. 221.

214 It is common for the Civil Rights era in American history, roughly *Brown* to the *Voting Rights Act*, to be referred to as the Second Reconstruction.

215 McPherson, James M. "Southern Comfort." *The New York Review of Books*, April 12, 2001.

216 Matthews, Dylan. "A basic income really could end poverty forever." *Vox*. July 17, 2017. https://www.vox.com/policy-and-politics/2017/7/17/15364546/universal-basic-income-review-stern-murray-automation.

## About the Author

DAVID FARIS is the author of *Dissent and Revolution in a Digital Age: Social Media, Blogging and Activism in Egypt*, the co-editor of *Social Media in Iran: Politics and Society After 2009*, and a regular contributor to *The Week*. He holds a PhD in political science from the University of Pennsylvania and is associate professor of political science at Roosevelt University in Chicago.